Live the Life You Want – A Guide to Following Your Dream, Fulfilling Your
Potential, and Becoming More.

Johnathan Laing

I believe sincerely that everyone I have met has played a part in creating this book, as they have made me who I am today. There are too many people to thank, to simply fit them on this page.

That being said, I would like to say a special thank you to my Aunty Ann, who literally changed my life at 13 years old and put me on course to live the life I want.

Without her help, love, support and inspiration I wouldn't be who I am today or have the endless possibilities to continue dreaming of becoming more than what I am.

Introduction

Firstly, thank you for taking the time to read this book. I want to tell you briefly why I've written it.

In a nutshell I hope that it helps you live the life you want.

I hope it does this by providing you with inspiration and reflection, as well as practical advice on actions you can undertake in order to achieve your goals and dreams.

As much as I do hope the book inspires you, I also hope it helps you act, to make your dreams come true. This will take some work. So at the end of each chapter I will ask you to reflect on what you have learned and respond to it with a plan of action.

Following whatever action you take I want you to note down the results of your efforts. This process, on repeat, is a vital part of achieving your dreams, living the life you want and fulfilling your potential.

For continued daily inspiration feel free to follow me on Twitter @wantingmoreltd, and find me on Facebook.

chapter
ONE

Why are you reading this book?

OK – so you have dreams of becoming more than you are today. You're reading this book because you want to achieve a dream or goal and need a little help on how to get there.

It could be that you have a very specific goal or dream in mind and you're struggling on how to realise it, or it could be that you don't know what you want.

You cannot escape a nagging feeling inside of wanting more. A feeling that you are not quite living the life you want.

Firstly, fantastic on having a desire to become more than what you are today, and don't concern yourself too much if you're not fully sure as to what it is you want, we will explore that in a bit more detail later.

Equally, if you have a very specific goal and are struggling to realise it, hopefully I can help there too.

You have amazing potential, and you have the ability to live the life you want. A lot of it comes down to the choices that you make.

Life is full of choices. Everyday we are presented with choices to make, and this has been happening all our lives. Since we were born we have been presented with choices, with options, with possibilities. And, as we grow older, the choices get bigger.

You cannot escape a nagging feeling inside of wanting more.

A feeling that you are not quite living the life you want.

Choosing a vocation, a career, a job, is one of the biggest choices you have to make in your life. Yet many people don't choose, at least not actively. They fall into a job, because they need one and, once inside, they fall into another job, perhaps a promotion, and so on.

It was *right in front* of them but not necessarily *right for* them.

It doesn't fit them, it doesn't feel right, they feel like they were destined for something different, something more, something better. But they don't do anything about it, because their dream – the thing they would really love to do – isn't being presented to them as a choice.

We get into the habit of waiting for choices to be presented to us: someone else gives you a "choice", but that choice is limited – someone else decides your options.

Choosing your own options can be daunting and difficult as we've been conditioned to go with the "realistic" option. But the "realistic" choice tends to amount to far less than we could actually achieve. "Realistic" also cushions and protects us from disappointment and failure.

The problem is, that in our desire to avoid disappointment in our lives, we end up with disappointing lives. You can avoid failure all your life, if you want, but you'll also avoid winning.

The vast majority of those who have achieved any degree of success or satisfaction in their lives have refused to let others limit their choices; they have accepted that to try / fail / try again was the only possibility.

Don't limit your options, possibilities and choices by outsourcing them, whether that's to your boss, to the job pages, or even worse, to the lottery ticket. Most people who have a dream of a better life don't realise that the probability of them achieving that is far greater than the odds of the lotto ticket they buy each week, hoping it will deliver them a better life.

Don't be limited by other people's options, create your own.

Decide what you want to do and do it. I know you have a lot of reasons why you can't, but some of those may be reasons imposed on you by others, some will be borne from fear, many I'm sure will involve the phrase "in reality".

Don't be limited by other people's options – create your own!

But the "reality" is this: it's your life, your time, your happiness, your choice.

Sounds simple when put like that, and it is easier to write it down then put it into action. After all, there's always something you must do that will get in the way, you have that in common with all other human beings. There is always something more important to do.

Seven and a half billion human beings exist right now. Our hearts beat the same. We all look up at the same sky and see the same stars, the same moon. We all live in the same time: right now. One other thing unites and binds us all together, no matter what our race, religion or location: every one of us, right now, has something to do. Even if that something is 'doing nothing'.

Right now someone is choosing a wedding dress, someone is choosing the starter for their meal, someone is quitting their job, someone has to decide whether to forgive an unfaithful partner, someone is putting fuel in their car, someone is giving birth, someone is being born, someone is reading a book, someone is looking for shoes to go with their outfit, someone is working out where their next meal will come from, someone is wondering how they will make it through the night… From the momentous to the mundane… the list of activities is, well, seven and a half billion long.

So, you have something to do. Sometimes it's unpleasant. Sometimes it's dull. Sometimes it makes you smile. Sometimes it makes you feel like every fibre in your being is exactly where it is meant to be right now. Sometimes you realise that these times are the ones that matter. These times. This time. Right now…

Whatever it is you have to do right now, make sure you are doing it because you *want* to.

Although human life expectancy is getting longer– life is still short. In relation to the age of the universe, human life barely exists at all. Is the something you have to do right now *really* what you want to do? (Aside, of course, from reading this book. Do please read on…)

If you're setting the alarm on a Sunday night whilst updating Facebook with another meme about how Monday can just 'do one', exactly what are getting up for? Surely Monday has nothing to do with it. Aren't you getting up for you? Are you doing what you have to do right now for you?

Possibly yes, probably no.

We all have commitments. We all have things that have to be done. Some of us more than most. It's sometimes hard to accept, but in most cases the reactions to our circumstances are a choice. I've been there, perhaps more than most. One Monday morning, many years ago, I was so desperately unhappy about the job I was going to, I actually contemplated crashing the car on the way to work. Not a bad crash, but just enough to get me off work for a couple of weeks.

It took some time for me to realise the difference between what I HAD to do and what I WANTED to do. So start by asking yourself the following three questions – they should help you begin to identify the differences between "have to do" and "want to do":

Why am I doing it?
Who am I doing it for?
How is it helping me live the life I want to live?

The atoms that make up your body were created 13.5 billion years ago. If you're lucky you'll get to use them for about 80 years or so. And the universe is set to go on for another TRILLION years or so. Just pause for a short moment. Think on that. To exist at all is such a fabulously amazing gift.

I expect, by the fact that you're reading this book, that you are probably not in your dream job? You might find your current job frustrating, dull, meaningless. It might be OK-ish, but doesn't exactly feel like you're "living the dream". Maybe you want a better job? Or it could be that you are doing your dream job and want to take it to the next level, that's great, I'm a fan of always "Wanting More".

What is your ideal job? What would make it better than your current role?

How we feel about our job has a massive impact on how well we perform in them. It's one of the many reasons businesses have strategies to engage their employees. It is also a self-repeating cycle; if you feel good about your job you are generally better at it – if you are good at your job you generally feel good.

So if you're not feeling too good about your job right now, what would be better?

Better is an interesting concept when you start to dig beneath it. "Better" is dependent on each individual's circumstances, and that can lead to some internal conflict.

Let's start with how you feel: surely a better job would be one that you find more enjoyable? But what if the better job paid you significantly less than what you earn today? Of course, happiness isn't about material reward, but if it meant that you couldn't maintain your current lifestyle, could you do it?

Clearly some people do – they quit their jobs and pursue their passion, accepting that it means curtailing their spending habits and living a more frugal, but happier, life. Of course, some of those people may have already achieved financial freedom before making a change. They've realised that the pursuit of material wealth isn't making them happy and it's time to stop amassing things they don't need.

But sometimes the lifestyle that we want to maintain isn't an extravagant one, but the "better job" isn't sufficient to pay the bills. But is that what you are living for? To pay bills?

Was your childhood aspiration to grow up and pay bills?

Take a look at your lifestyle and possessions: your house, your car, all your "stuff"; would you be willing to sacrifice it all for that better job? Is it all worth mortgaging your happiness until you retire? It's a serious question you must ask yourself. If you are not willing to sacrifice even some (not all) of your stuff for a "better job" then stop longing for it.

Realise that you are happy with what you have and work on enjoying your job. It's giving you the lifestyle you want and you're going in and working at it every day, so you may as well choose to enjoy it. And the more you enjoy it, the more successful you will become.

Choose to enjoy your job and you will be better at your job.

Or, be willing to free yourself from the "stuff" that you've accumulated. Downsize, reduce, reclaim your happiness! Unlock your potential to wake up every day feeling excited about what you do for a living. Do the better job and have a better life.

The choice is yours. Don't pretend to feel trapped in your own life.

Don't allow yourself to sit in a state of longing for something that you do nothing about. You are creating your own misery. Embrace what you have and start enjoying it, or start working on transforming your life.

The choice is yours.

Don't pretend to feel trapped in your own life.

You want a "better job"? Well, you can have one – it just might be the one you're doing right now.

If you're certain it's not, and you know you want more then think about how you get that. One of the ways I've developed myself over the years is by taking what I'm good at, and becoming better. Sharpening my edge.

Most of us have things we are good at and things we are not so good at. Areas where we sparkle and shine and those where we stumble and struggle. Strengths and weaknesses.

In the work environment, many people find themselves assigned a personal development plan by their line manager. For some it will be a brief 'tick box' exercise during an annual performance review, and for some it will be reviewed more regularly. I've observed that on many occasions these development plans focus solely on what needs to be improved on, the stuff we're not very good at. The weaknesses.

But when that's the case, we're missing the chance to turn the good stuff into the really great stuff. To hone a skill.

To sharpen the edge.

Let's be realistic, a lot of the time the things we are not very good at are also the things we don't like. Whilst it's good to stretch and spend time outside your comfort zone, there may be some skills, tasks or roles that you will never really enjoy and that you will never be very good at. No matter how much work you put in, you'll never become more than mediocre because, quite simply, your heart isn't in it.

In the meantime, the stuff we are *really* skilled in – the stuff we really enjoy and display a real talent for – gets neglected.

Development plans should focus on growing, and gaining more skills, but there should be space within them to focus on the areas we are already good at and become great at them. That's where we stand the best chance of becoming truly exceptional.

Imagine the potential within a workforce where every individual's talents were nurtured to an exceptional level. Consider what such a group could achieve!

Of course we should be aware of our development areas – that's a fundamental element of developing your skills in areas that you're not so good at. But that aside, wouldn't it be fantastic to have the chance to take what you're good at and become even better – to become 'world famous' for it?

I consider my biggest strength – my talent – to be motivating and inspiring others. It's something I'm good at, it's something I'm passionate about doing and it's something I enjoy with every fibre of my being. It's also something I continue to focus on becoming better at. I still consider myself to be an apprentice in the subject, pursuing an ongoing learning journey. I'm committed to move from being good at it, to being great at it. I'm focused on becoming 'world famous' for it.

The world's top sport professionals, musicians, writers, leaders and artists all apply a daily focus to their talent and work on becoming even better at it.

No matter what the field, those who are at the top of their game continue to practice and push themselves to do more. To be more.

I encourage everyone to take time to think about what you really love, what you feel you are really good at. Then make it your aim to become really, truly great. Yes, be mindful of the stuff you aren't good at – manage it as a risk, seek out a team or collaborate with individuals whose talents support yours.

Don't allow development plans to focus primarily on the negatives. Use them to celebrate your strengths and channel your attention and energy on taking those areas from good to great. And then from great to magnificent…

Allow your talent to shine so brightly it illuminates the way to the life you want to live.

By cultivating our strengths, we tap into potential opportunities that we may be unable to imagine right now.

So, let the world know what you're good at. Don't wait for someone else to set you a development plan – start sharpening your edge now.

An important point, however, is not to worry if you feel you don't have something you're good at, just focus on what you enjoy doing. You have it within you to achieve great success, but maybe you've combined it with a job or activities that are not helping you. Even if you don't feel it right now, there is a fire within you, within us all, there's even fire in water.

Water is a truly amazing, incredible thing. An ice-cold drink, a warm bath, the gentle sound of the sea lapping on the shore, water is all around us. Where there is water there is life; water is the essential ingredient for all life as we know it.

Of course it's not just essential for nourishing and sustaining life, it is also extremely good at putting out fires. So it's always fascinated me that the substance we use to put out fires is made of two highly combustible elements – hydrogen and oxygen.

In isolation hydrogen and oxygen are very combustible: in fact if you put them together under enough pressure you have an explosive force so powerful it will push a rocket out into space. As the hydrogen and oxygen explode into water the molecules hit the inside top of the fuel tank and push the rocket upwards. It's that simple... it's rocket science (literally).

When we're in contact with water it's difficult to comprehend the sheer scale of the explosive, fiery energy that it contains. Of course water itself isn't flammable, only when you break it down and separate the elements. So, depending on the conditions, it contains the power to extinguish or propel.

Similarly we all contain fire: our passion, the thing that drives us and that we love and feel alive when doing...

But as hydrogen and oxygen can combine to extinguish fire, the same thing can happen to our internal fires, to our passions. You may have combined your passion with a job you don't like, you may have combined your passion with a skewed perception that you have no time, you may have combined it with passive habits that work against your passion.

To give your "fire" a chance you might have to think about separating it from the elements that are getting in the way, you might have to start making active choices rather than getting swept along with the currents of passive habits.

Otherwise the sparks of passion will amount to nothing and will fizzle out before they have a chance. Are you developing the conditions to produce a force that propels or a force that extinguishes?

You can't set fire to water, but under the right conditions the elements within it could put you on the moon. Are you creating the right conditions to unleash that kind of fire?

When considering what you want with your life, I would encourage you to think big.

Whilst recently watching the movie "Stranger Than Fiction" I heard the following line: "Let's start at ridiculous and move backwards". I loved this quote and the idea that it represents – it reminded me of how we can all too often begin any form of endeavour by starting at "sensible".

We've become conditioned to play it safe, to avoid risks, to side-step adventure.

When it comes to what you want in life, I'd encourage you all to ditch sensible and start at ridiculous. From there you can work backwards to figure out how you can make 'ridiculous' happen. And so what if it seems ridiculous? So what if it seems unreasonable? So what if it seems audacious?

I've seen so many individuals who were taught from an early age to constantly lower their expectations, so they didn't wind up being disappointed with the outcome. Fair enough, but I'd like to suggest that there are worse things in life than being disappointed because your dream was too big.

We've become conditioned to play it safe, to avoid risks, to side-step adventure.

Don't accept mediocrity; reject requests to lower your expectations. Allow yourself to dream big.

It was ridiculous that in 1454 a German goldsmith had the idea to build the world's first printing press when ninety six percent of the population couldn't read.

The Wright brothers were thinking audaciously when they began building their first flying machine.

Steve Jobs' idea of a device smaller than the size of an audio cassette yet capable of holding an individual's entire music collection seemed completely unreasonable.

These individuals had bold, brave and unreasonable ideas, but they pursued them nonetheless. And we're all glad that they did.

Those with ridiculous, audacious and unrealistic ideas are often the individuals who are bold and brave enough to push beyond the sensible, safe and acceptable boundaries to deliver products, services or concepts that others would have never even allowed themselves to imagine.

Don't hold yourself back, don't settle for less, don't be put off by others who may laugh or scorn your ideas. Be bold. Be brave. Be unreasonable.

Start at ridiculous, and move backwards.

At this stage I feel it's appropriate to give you a little warning. Having bold dreams are great, having any type of goal or aspiration for more is something I believe makes for a better life. But it comes at a price.

I want an apartment in the Plaza Hotel in New York City.

They don't come cheap, and I need to increase my income considerably in the next five years to make that happen (I gave myself a specific date). The Plaza apartment is just one of my big, audacious, scary, exciting, ridiculous dreams.

Big dreams come with a cost, but I'm not just talking about the obvious financial cost.

I mean the cost to you now.

If you have big dreams – material, career, artistic, personal, however you want to define them – whatever those dreams are they come at a cost. They have a price.

The cost is your time and what you are willing to sacrifice to achieve it. If you want to be an actor you need to work on your craft every single day – learning lines, breaking down scenes or exploring new techniques. If you want to be a writer you need to put pen to paper / fingers to keyboard every single day. If you want to be the company CEO then on a daily basis you need to add more value to the business, build more bridges between people and departments and do it all better than everyone else.

If you have big dreams then the cost of achieving them has to be felt now. If you're not feeling it, if you don't feel that everything you do is pushing towards and supporting your dreams, then perhaps it's never going to happen.

And for many people, it won't. Simply because they're not willing to face up to the cost of their dreams today.

But right now, you have the same opportunity to achieve your big dreams as everyone else; the same opportunity as those who are achieving the same kind of dreams (and bigger) that you have.

The bottom line is this: having big dreams isn't going to be easy, and at times you will feel like giving up, at times it will feel impossible. The cost is making a commitment, and being sure that nothing will get in the way of making that dream come true.

Are you ready to pay that price?

I mentioned above about my desire for a Plaza apartment, let me tell you a little bit more about myself. From an early age I've always wanted more, more for my life, my dreams, my goals. It isn't about accumulation of material things and obsessive desires to have significant' amounts of wealth. Don't get me wrong, I personally don't see any issue with people who do want to achieve financial freedom to do what they want with their life, but after a certain point, accumulation of money will not deliver anymore happiness.

There is nothing wrong with wanting to be in profit, every human being wants to have more money coming in than they have going out. We live in a world where we have infinite desires and finite resources. But having money, having a collection of "things" and getting more and more "stuff" in your life will not make you happy in isolation.

It is important to know what you are doing it for, as in understanding what is driving the desire behind your dreams and goals. I will explore this later, but sometimes what we think our dreams are can be misplaced. We have been taught to attach certain material values to our achievements, and by understanding the real driving force behind your dreams, what it is you are really looking to fulfil in your life, you will be able to ensure you direct your actions to achieve true happiness.

What I don't want you to do is work on achieving a dream to find that it doesn't deliver the happiness you expected – which can be more common than you realise.

I grew up in a reasonably poor neighbourhood and family, the outlook on life from an early age was rather bleak. The industry in my town was in significant decline, with the main source of jobs coming from coal mining and factory work, both of which were increasingly being reduced and replaced by overseas cheaper production and labour.

The prospect of leaving school at 16 and never working was a very real one when I looked around the neighbourhood I lived in.

I remember from an early age feeling uncomfortable with this, I must have only been around 11 years old. I didn't want that life, I wanted more.

This was not easy and sometimes caused tension with my family as I appeared to be acting "above my station", by wanting more for my life I was rejecting the life of the people around me.

That was not easy.

This tension came to a head when I was 13 and moved out and into foster care with my aunt. It was the break I needed to start working on becoming more than what I was, and more than what others felt I was destined to become.

Sometimes as we go through our lives we are forced to make choices, some of them small ones, some of them significantly larger, but whatever the size of the choice it is important to recognise that these choices have the power to drive us towards the life we want to live, or sometimes to the one we don't want to live.

Our circumstances, on the whole, are a reflection of the choices we've made in our lives.

As a child I remember dreaming of a better life, and soon these dreamed turned into tangible goals. I remember wanting to have a detached house with a black leather sofa in the living room (sometimes our dreams can be very specific!). I have no idea why, but in my mind at the time it represented a certain style of living that I aspired to, and I am proud to say I achieved it.

I remember on another occasion talking to my friend about wanting to stay in the Plaza hotel in New York City, at the time he reminded me that my head was always in the clouds and that people "like us" don't stay in the Plaza Hotel.

In 2003 I did stay in the Plaza, and it was literally a dream come true. Earlier I mentioned I wanted a Plaza apartment, that's because they've now converted most of the hotel into apartments. So I have a new goal. At this stage I haven't worked out all the detail of how I am going to do it, in the same way that when I was 12 and dreamt of staying in the Plaza I had no idea how I was going to make it happen.

All I knew then, and all I know now – is that I did and I will make it happen.

This drive and ambition for me to achieve my goals and dreams is what motivates me to become more than what I am today. It helps get through the tough days, whether it is work or life in general that is making it tough. It pushes me to go outside my comfort zone.

It creates a desire to learn and improve, it makes me question the questions as well as the answers.
It creates an insatiable desire for more.

It is important to recognise that it is not the achievement of the goal itself that makes me happy, getting to the Plaza, or having a detached house, black sofa and Jaguar car doesn't make me happy. It is the fact that I can do these things, that I can push myself and surprise myself with how much I can do, how much I can change, and this makes me happy.

It excites me just how many possibilities there are in the world.

"The more I learn, the more I realise how much I don't know", is a quote from Einstein. I find this incredibly inspirational, it is not about attaining knowledge, it is about attaining more questions, more possibilities, more problems to solve.

Answers can be boring, and final, they represent the end, the conclusion. Once a problem has been solved, once you have a solution, there can be an anti-climax, a "now what?" moment.

This can be the same with your goals and dreams, why it's always important to realise that it isn't about the final destination, the solution, the end.

This is the essence of my desire for wanting more, and why I set up a company called Wanting More!

Along my journey so far I've learned a lot, failed a lot, tried a lot, failed to understand, questioned myself, been upset with myself, been overwhelmed at times, been under-whelmed at times, been the happiest I've ever been and the sometimes the saddest I've ever been.

I've experienced fear like I never thought I would but at the same time I've achieved things I thought were almost impossible just 20 years ago.

And I'm not finished, and by no way perfect. There are still goals and dreams that allude me, still some aspects of my life that I am working on changing and it isn't easy.

Some of the really important dreams we have are hard work, and if they could be achieved with the simple click of a finger, then life wouldn't be that interesting.

It is OK to struggle with your goals, I have ones I'm still struggling with, but that doesn't make me give up on them.

Remember that having the solution, the answer, isn't always the best place to be!

There is no right and wrong when it comes to living your life, no perfect solution. The main thing to remember is that it is your life to live, which means that you get to do what you want with it, even if sometimes it feels like you don't.

As I've shaped and changed my own life into the life I want, I've also helped others do the same. That is the intention I have with this book, I want to share some of my experience and thoughts with the desire to help others on their journey of achieving their dreams.

I want to help you to dream more, to do more and ultimately become more than what you are today.

Remember:
having the
solution,
the answer,
isn't always
the best
place to be!

Be under no illusion, personal transformation is not easy and at times you will question whether you really want your dreams, whether they are really worth it.

As I said earlier, I'm not done yet myself, some of my dreams still cause some significant discomfort, especially in taking full ownership for their achievement.

Becoming more, living the life you want and achieving your dreams can be very complex. Often the action to achieve them can be simple, but we are complex beings, who don't seem to make decisions in our own best interest. We also seem to have a habit of making choices that are not aligned to our future goals.

Because of this complexity I've broken down the process into three stages. Dream, Do, Become.

The first three chapters explore the concept of dreaming, helping you to understand where to start. It is fine not to have a defined goal in mind at this moment in time, I hope to help you with that. We will dig deep into your dreams and goals to understand what is really important so that we ensure you are aiming for the right thing.

The middle part of the book explores the concept of "do more", how to put your goals and dreams into action. How to respond to failing (which you will do at some points), how to build a new habit, how to let go and realise what you are willing to sacrifice to achieve your dreams.

The final part of the book will focus on "be more", what it is like to live a transformed life, ensuring you unlock your full potential, keeping it going and how to start the process again.

I'm excited by the unlimited possibilities ahead of us as we go on this journey together. As I continue my personal transformation you can follow me on twitter, read my blog and let me know how you are getting on with your own transformation.

So, if you are ready for wanting more, let's get started.

Chapter One – the three Rs...

Reflect:

How do you feel? Do you feel trapped? Frustrated? Do you feel that you have more potential than what you are displaying right now? Do you feel you are worth more than your current circumstances demonstrate? Do you want more?

Respond:

Are you prepared to be open and positive about the possibilities contained in your own life? Are you prepared to act on your dreams? Set yourself a plan to remain positive and open to the potential as you read the book. If you've read the first chapter and feel it's not for you, then put it down and live your life. But if you do want more, if you want to live the life you want, set yourself a plan of action now to commit to it.

Result:

This bit you get to come back to. I want you to note down what the results are of you being open to the idea that you can achieve the success you want. Keep coming back to this as a reminder to remain open and committed to achieving your dreams.

chapter
TWO

Dream
More

We normally associate the word dreaming with what we do when we are asleep – or in the case of "day-dreaming" a term that means your mind is wondering, taking you away from the here and now.

Lately the term dreaming has become associated closely with goals and aspirations.

Dreams are a very powerful part of achieving a goal, or changing something in your life. They help you form a vision in your mind of what it is you want to achieve.

As I mentioned in the introduction, when I was much younger I dreamed about going to NYC and staying in the Plaza hotel, I imagined what it would be like to be in a New York cab asking the driver to take me to the Plaza, what it would be like checking in, and walking down the corridor to my room.

Whilst my dream also included a suite over-looking Central Park and the reality was a standard room overlooking the side street, the dream was a very important part of keeping my goal alive, especially when it seemed far away.

Dreaming is about taking yourself out of the here and now, in a good way. It is about a future state in which you have become something more. Dreaming has no limits, in our dreams we can do what we want, be who we want and achieve what we want.

That's what makes dreams so wonderful, and why they are a really important part of aspiring to be more than what you are today.

In order to dream more you have to let go of the restrictions your mind places on the here and now. Whenever we start to dream of a better life our mind tends to remind of us things such as, the mortgage needs paying, the bills, the food, the fuel for the car, the kids university fees, the lack of time, the lack of energy, the skill etc.

All these things are relevant and cannot be dismissed. They are real concerns and issues that press on our minds. At the same time, you probably already feel that a lot of the concerns and "reasons" for not achieving what you want in life don't feel that important. By that I mean they are important of course, paying your bills, maintaining a home, a family etc are very important. But they don't feel that they are the purpose for living.

Part of dreaming, however, is a willingness to let go of these things, to clear your mind and enter a state in which you allow yourself to dream about what you really want, and not being afraid to dream big.

It could be that your dream of a better life involves working for yourself, perhaps you've got an idea for something new, something never seen before, something the world doesn't even know it wants or needs just yet. You may possess that rare and amazing thing, an original idea. You have no way of knowing if it will work, but the idea persists.

When it comes to original ideas, the line between insane or inspired can be very thin.

As a $100 billion company, the idea behind Facebook is inspired but imagine someone trying to explain the concept to you just 15 years ago – it would have probably seemed insane… updating our lives on our phones and computers for everyone to see? Telling people when you're in a restaurant or what you're watching on TV or sharing pictures of your children or pets.

Perhaps to some people the concept still seems insane, but clearly for many the idea works – it's inspired. Because it's what we know. How brilliant that we can all share in each others' lives. It's great that friends can see my holiday photos and actually comment on them, whilst I'm still on holiday!

I mentioned previously about the printing press being invented around the year 1440. At that time, about 96% of the world's population couldn't read and, of those who could, many didn't have the means to purchase a book! It surely seems insane to invent something that is practically of no use to the vast majority of human beings on the planet? Of course we know now that it was inspired, not insane.

We know *now*… but it's often impossible to know *then*…

Hindsight can be a wonderful learning tool and a regrettable menace at the same time.

Pursuing something – an idea for an invention, a new job opportunity, a change in your life direction – all require determination, passion, belief and possibly a little splash of arrogance. It requires a little bit of arrogance to believe that your idea will work, when the world around you, the people around you, believe that your idea (and, perhaps by association, you) to be insane.

And of course, it could be, which is why I cautiously advise only a splash of arrogance. We all must accept at some point that our crazy idea, that no one else has ever thought of, is really a crazy idea. But that shouldn't stop us from trying. As the world changes and develops there will be more and more changes that bring about opportunities for new ideas to flourish.

So embrace your creativity – exercise it! The more you use it the more powerful it becomes and the more ideas you will have. Get excited and inspired by those 'spark' moments. And make sure that you get your ideas out there, share them with people around you.

But always accept that the line between insane and inspired is thin. Get comfortable with the notion that along the way you will walk on both sides of that line. If an idea doesn't work then let it go, let it 'fall by the wayside', but make sure you take the occasional trip to the 'wayside'. What seems insane now, may be accepted as inspired tomorrow – your idea may have just been ahead of its time.

But, equally, do not panic if you don't have an original idea, they are rare things. It's most likely that you're dreams and aspirations are a variation on something someone else has done before.

Creating original content can be very hard, no matter what your field. Whether it's writing, composing, leading a business or even inventing, chances are someone has done it before you.

This makes for challenging times, as everyone is trying to bring something new to market, trying to say something original, trying to tell a new story.

It's not impossible to be the creator of something truly original, but it's rare.

The narratives of most films can be traced back to stories in Shakespeare, which in turn echo folk tales that were passed down from generation to generation for hundreds of years, long before Shakespeare was born.

Your dreams, your goals, your aspirations, it's likely someone has gone before you and done it already. Does this mean you shouldn't bother? Of course not. There's nothing wrong with a "cover version". The beauty I encourage you to embrace is that you already have your originality – you.

There is only one of you.

Don't obsess about creating new content, don't concern yourself with embarking on goals that may be a variation on a theme already explored by someone else.

That was them, and this is you.

Get to know your voice, get to know who you are and what you want. Imprint yourself on whatever it is you want to do with your life, and you will have originality. You will have uniqueness. You will have something that's never been seen before – because you've not been before.

Now is your time to shine like a star, to put yourself forward and embrace your uniqueness. Be the best you that you can be.

Don't hold back on yourself, don't hesitate and question whether you can do it. Whilst you're waiting to decide, you are losing time.

You have nothing to lose living life on your terms.

Tell the story your way. Dance down the path that others walked. Sing a cover version.

Be brave, be bold, be you and be now.

The dreaming I want you to do to establish your goals, is to allow yourself not to be restricted by mental blockers, but still to be in the realm of physical reality. What do I mean by this? In dreams when you sleep, you can fly and do all sorts of things that defy logic and physics, in the type of dreaming I'm referring to you will retain your grip on the laws of physics.

If your dream is to fly like superman, this book cannot help you with that!

You may dream, however, of being a writer, an actor, a CEO of a company, of having a healthier body, playing a

You have nothing to lose living life on your terms.

musical instrument or of owning a Manhattan apartment. These are things humans do, they may be things you want to do and your mind has put up mental barriers as to why you can't, or even discarded the dream altogether.

It may be, like many people, that you dream of winning the lottery. I would suggest caution in relation to this type of dreaming, the odds are stacked against you, though I do understand the desire for the huge windfalls the lottery promises.

A while ago UK's National Lottery organisers changed how the game worked and, in doing so, they decreased the odds of winning from 1 in 14 million to 1 in 49 million, at the same time they doubled the price of a ticket. They took this decision as, over the course of some years, ticket sales had been on a constant decline.

But the decision to increase ticket sales by decreasing the odds of winning and increasing the price seems counter intuitive to most. After all, why would people be more inclined to buy a ticket if they knew their chances of winning had significantly decreased and it was costing them more?

The truth – one that the National Lottery's organisers factored into their decision – is that we tend to be more attracted to bigger wins, even if the odds of winning are increasingly unlikely. As the odds of winning decreased significantly the amount of "no win" jackpots lead to bigger roll-over draws and much bigger prizes.

It seems that the attraction of winning 1 or 2 million pounds is not as big a draw as winning 30 or 50 million pounds, regardless of the odds. Perhaps these days people dream more of being a billionaire than a millionaire!

We have a tendency for such "over dreaming" in so many aspects of our lives. People are attracted to the "crash" diets that promise a twelve pound loss in a week instead of the sustainable, if somewhat less dramatic, activities that will yield a one pound loss each week. And let's face it, achieving a result in one week that would otherwise take three months does sound attractive. But whether such results are sustainable is another question…

The same applies with other goals in our lives.

It's great to have big, scary, audacious goals, but the reality is that you achieve them by achieving lots of small goals along the way.

Sometimes the big goals can get in the way. They can seem so huge that they appear to be more dream-like than a tangible goal. Like winning the lottery, they become highly unlikely and more to do with random chance.

Luckily, your life is not a game of chance. Your life is a result of your actions, your choices and the small goals that you achieve each and every day. The small goals which at the time seem to have so little bearing on the large ones.

Striking the balance between "over-dreaming" and "dreaming big" can be a difficult one. Be careful of the attraction of the big prize with unlikely odds, and focus instead on the small, daily wins.

Taken in isolation, a single breath seems insignificant. But our lives depend on every single breath we take.

In the same way, our goals and dreams are achieved and realised through the actions we take every single day. Don't lose sight of that.

One of the reasons we get attracted to the highly unlikely is because of what we see around us, we see people living lives we want to live. And of course, people do win the lottery, thousands of people have become overnight multi-millionaires. They're the lucky ones, sometimes it seems that luck can evade those who don't win. Will we ever get lucky?

It seems like some people get all the luck. You know the ones – those who are always two steps ahead in life and business?

What if you could generate your own luck? Wouldn't that be worth knowing how to do? An article in The Harvard Business Review identified three key traits exhibited by many 'lucky' entrepreneurs and business leaders.

Taken in isolation, a single breath seems insignificant. But our lives depend on every single breath we take.

But these behaviours can apply to anyone who wants to 'make their own luck', whether in life, love or business.

Humility

The first step towards generating a lucky attitude is humility. Humility doesn't exclude self-belief, self-confidence, drive or ambition – you need those traits to motivate yourself and inspire others. But you must be humble enough to accept that you don't know everything.

As Michael Dell once advised: "Try never to be the smartest person in the room. And if you are, I suggest you invite smarter people... or find a different room". Surround yourself with friends, colleagues and mentors who you can learn from, and never be afraid to ask for their assistance or input. Doing this will help foster the second trait...

Curiosity

Being continually interested in new ideas, experiences and skills is an important way to ensure you don't become arrogant or find your views stagnating. There's a great quote from Eleanor Roosevelt which sums up the inherent value contained within curiosity: "If a mother could ask a fairy godmother to endow it with the most useful gift, that gift would be curiosity."

If you adopt the humble outlook outlined above you will be more inclined to learn from others. This in turn will widen the range of opportunities you get exposed to. The humble and the curious (AKA the 'lucky' ones) tend to encounter more opportunities than others, which in turn can lead to a greater sense of…

Optimism

We've all heard of the power of possessing a positive outlook and 'lucky' people tend to maintain a continually positive outlook on life. That's because sticking with a positive outlook will ultimately generate more positivity. Colin Powell once said that "perpetual optimism is a force multiplier" – in other words, the more optimism you generate the more you'll have to work with.

Optimists are more inclined to act on their instincts or explore new pursuits. Furthermore, optimism is an attractive force which will draw other like-minded people to support the 'lucky' in their ventures.

So, roll with it…

As you can see, the behaviours needed to manifest your own 'luck' are really quite straightforward. These attributes are available, attainable and can be put into action by just about anyone.

So why not start today?

Begin with a foundation of humility. Then be curious and look beyond your own knowledge and experience. Finally, be optimistic that you are going to be successful.

Because the chances are you will be.

Your dreams, goals and aspirations are not down to chance, you're not buying a lottery ticket or rolling the dice to see where they land. You do, however, need to think about how important the dream is to you, how do you know that it is really what you want?

We will explore in the coming chapters how to test if your dream is really what you want and how achievable it is, but for now let's start by considering some questions. You may want to jot these down in a pad, a notebook or journal, or if you're like me and have gone paperless and reading this as an e-book, then you should be able to make notes in the e-book itself! Both Kindle and i-books have this functionality, though personally I find it easier in i-books.

Don't concern yourself if you don't have the answers to these questions immediately, some of them will take time to consider. You may choose to jot down your initial thoughts and come back to them as you reflect more.

When you were younger, what was your dream job? What did you want to be when you "grew up"?

What is most important to you?

What do you want to achieve in the next, 12 months, 5 years, lifetime?

When you go to sleep at night, what you do you hope and pray for the next day?

What do you want people to say about you when you leave the room?

What do you want people to say about you when you're gone forever?

What about the following do you want to change:

- Your life?
- Your body?
- Your mind?
- Your relationship(s)?
- Your work?
- Your habits?
- Your hobbies?
- Your time?

There are other questions to ask, but I'm sure you'll agree, these are pretty big questions. The answers are not something that will be easily completed in a few minutes. They are questions I've been asking myself for many years, it helps to keep coming back to them, and accepting that the answers develop, change and grow as you change develop and grow.

So why dream? Why is this important? Isn't it just another way of setting a goal?

The reason I use dream and not goal at this stage is that I believe all our goals start with a dream. And in a dream we allow ourselves to be more unlimited than we do when setting goals, when our minds tend to be "realistic" and sometimes down-grades what we want to achieve.

Dreaming takes us back to what we believed in when we were growing up, which was an unlimited sense of potential.

As a child learning about the world around us we get a sense of it's true awesomeness and potential. Children have no problems dreaming about all the possibilities that lie ahead.

Children do not have the same mind blockers that we get as an adult, they haven't yet learnt to limit themselves. Perhaps because they've not experienced the disappointment of dreams not coming true.

The main key difference between a dream and a goal is that a goal is a dream with a deadline, so it tends to be more practical, whereas a dream is more about your vision.

I will discuss goals more in the "Do More" section, for now it's important that you keep an open mind about the possibilities that are in front of you.

Dreaming was so important to me when I was growing up. I created in my mind the potential for me to become more than what I was. I refused to accept certain restrictions that were placed on my life due to circumstance. The first 13 years of my life were pretty bumpy, I spent time moving in and out of my home.

My home life was not stable and through the choices of my older brother and mother (no father around) I was presented with a future view of the world that I didn't accept.

I didn't want a world that involved drugs, no work, being in trouble with the police, not attending school, constantly looking for someone else to blame for our circumstances. It was not the life I wanted.

I wanted more.

So I started dreaming. I started imagining what life could be like, what I wanted it to be like, how I wanted it to be. I started dreaming of all the future potential that was in front of me.

It forced me to make choices, difficult choices, such as leaving home at 13 and ending a destructive relationship with my family. Luckily for me I was rescued by my aunt, and wouldn't be here today if it wasn't for her help at such an important point in my life.

I recognise that as much as I am a strong believer in being focused on what you can do to help yourself and not blaming your circumstances entirely on external situations, other people do help you.

That is to say, the external situation you find yourself in does have a significant impact on your ability to achieve your goals and dreams.

Dreaming is the start.

Dreaming was the start point of my journey to wanting more and I'm still dreaming today.

I still want more.

DREAMING IS THE START

Hopefully you will see as you go through the book that it is something that never stops.

It might be something you have not done before, so starting with the questions earlier in the chapter is the first thing. Next we will explore your vision and purpose and how to dig into your dreams to ensure the action you work on is fully aligned with what you really want.

Chapter Two – the three Rs...

Reflect:

What is your dream? What do you want? What makes you really happy?

Respond:

Set an action plan to align your mood to the three elements of 'luck', Humility, Curiosity, Optimism. Stay focused on these three emotions, become aware of them. Stay focused as you continue to read this book, and throughout your day to day life.

Result:

In a few weeks make a note of how you feel. What was the result of staying focused on the above emotions?. Keep coming back to this, it isn't a one-time exercise. There are many distractions and life events that can pull you away from these emotions, which is why it's so important to keep coming back to them.

chapter
THREE

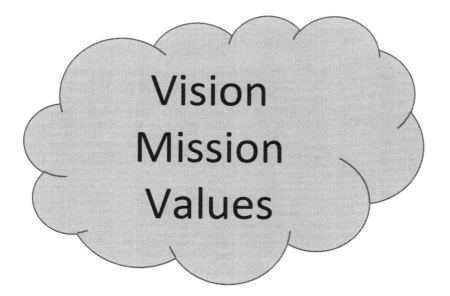

Vision
Mission
Values

It is vital to think about the vision of where you are going. This will enable you to dream long term and be fully focused on the future potential.

It is important to understand why you want something, as well as the thing itself.

I will explore in the next chapter more details about what sits behind your dreams, for now we want to focus on your vision and how realistic your dreams are.

Many businesses have vision statements, they describe the positive intended outcome of their strategy. They vary in size and impact, but they are all there to do the same thing. To describe in a succinct way what the company is about, what the company wants to achieve.

If you currently work for an organisation, it is highly likely they will have a vision statement, something that describes the overall purpose of what you are there to do. It could be something like "making a difference to everyday lives". It could be about putting "clear water between you and the competition".

Usually most vision statements provide a sense of purpose behind the daily tasks and activities, your objectives.

Businesses have these visions because they know how important that sense of purpose is. It is very easy to lose a sense of purpose when just focusing on tasks and activities.

It doesn't take long before people start questioning "exactly what are we doing this for?", what is the purpose, the meaning.

We crave purpose and meaning. It is why it is important not only in business, but in our personal lives as well.

My personal vision is to:

"Help people live the life they want, by enabling them to dream more, do more and become more".

This drives me, it drives what I do, it drives my behaviour. It is the energy underneath my passion for helping others. And of course, I can't help others live the life they want if I'm not doing it myself, so it reminds me of the choices I make to support my own goals and dreams.

As I mentioned in the introduction, I still have things I want to achieve, and some days are harder than others. But I'm not giving up, and I hope you don't too.

I know some of you may be thinking how does that vision relate to having a detached house, a black sofa and eventually an apartment in the Plaza? These things provide me with measurement of my success, they are not the goals in themselves, but evidence of living the life I want. Of progressing and achieving things beyond where I am at this point in my life.

Those measures grow and change over time, such as a five night stay in the Plaza turning into an apartment. Some of them are easier and smaller measures of success than others, but they are just measures of the success, not the success itself.

We will get onto some of your measures as we move into talking about the specific mission and goals you want to achieve.

For now take a moment to think about your own vision. What is the purpose of your life? How do you want to describe to someone the difference your life makes to the world, the people around you and most importantly, to yourself?

What matters to you the most? What is the most important thing in your life? What are you passionate about? What gets you out of bed early? What makes you want to go that extra mile?

It will take some time for you to consider it, my personal vision developed over a long period of time, as I started to realise that I was really passionate about helping people live the life they want.

I would find myself attracted to "coaching opportunities" of people I've worked with, sometimes people I'd only just met. I would want to know what they wanted to do with their life and immediately switch in to a conversation about how they make that happen. It was after realising that I loved those conversations that I got to my personal vision statement.

And remember that your vision doesn't have to contain the tangible specific goals, that is what your mission statement is for! Take a moment to jot down the answers to the above questions about what is important, what drives you, this is where you will get your vision from. As it may take time for it to develop don't stress about having a polished one line statement. Keep coming back to it as you work through the book.

So you've heard my vision, to help people live the life they want, here's my mission statement:

"To be a coach, author, trainer and world expert on cultural and individual transformation"

You will notice that it is definitely more specific and tangible in its outcome than the vision statement.

Think of the vision as the thing that guides what you do, your actions and behaviours. Your mission is the direction you are going in, it provides you with a constant opportunity to stop and evaluate if you are where you want to be right now and if you actions and behaviours are moving you in the right direction.

You will notice that my mission statement is still very bold and ambitious, because of this I haven't put a time scale on it. You can put a timescale on your mission, this will be determined based on how ambitious you decide your mission to be.

You don't have to have a mission to change the world, it's OK to have a desire to achieve something that is in the next 12 months, it can be good to start out a bit smaller and grow into it, adapt your vision and mission as you start to transform.

You may feel, and I often do, that mine is a little over-ambitious, but having big audacious goals works for me personally, for you they may not and that's OK.

This is not an issue.

It is your life, so it should be your mission, and it can be changed and adapted over time.

I regularly have a review of my own performance against my mission, in the same way that performance gets reviewed in a work setting. Sometimes if I am intensely working towards a goal I will have a review of how I'm doing on a weekly or monthly basis, for longer term goals I will review quarterly.

When setting your mission it can be difficult sometimes to understand how realistic it is, getting the balance between being audaciously bold and achievable is not easy. There is no exact science to it and personally I would lean more towards the bold and slightly un-achievable rather than something which is easily achieved.

I understand there will be differing opinions on this. Some people prefer to set small achievable goals, so that once achieved, they give a sense of purpose and celebration which helps when moving on to the next goal.

This makes perfect sense, and if that works for you – then go ahead and do it!

My main reason for encouraging people to be bold and set goals that they may not readily believe they can achieve, is because a lot of people tend to down-grade what they think they are capable of.

I believe that we are capable of achieving so much more than we realise. It doesn't mean it's easy, and sometimes along the way it will involve activity that hardly seems fun, but if you are in full pursuit of your dreams, then you will be living the life you want.

Only setting goals
that you know you
are certain to
achieve can lead to
an ever-decreasing
set of ambitions.

So how do you assess how achievable your goals are? One way to assess them is to think about how many other people have achieved the same goal. For example: if you want to be a writer, there are millions of people before you who have successfully written books and had them published. So therefore, it is entirely realistic that you could become a writer. The same could be said if you wanted to be an actor, own your own business, be an expert in your field etc etc.

A corresponding example, say you dream about going to the moon. Only 12 people have ever been to the moon. It doesn't make your dream impossible, but it does make achieving it less likely.

I'm not saying this to restrict your dreams, if you have a dream to achieve or do something that has never been done before, fabulous! Go ahead, everything has to start with the first person doing it!

Cars were invented before roads were built to carry them, people dreamed of flying machines long before anyone actually took off in one. In many countries women dreamed of the right to vote before they were able to.

Don't be afraid to dream of something no-one else has done before, it could be that you are in the right place at the right time to achieve something that others have previously thought impossible.

That said, establishing the numbers of previous people to have achieved your dream is a great starting point to get to grips with how realistic your goal is.

Knowing how realistic the goal is does not tell you how easy it will be to achieve. Whilst other people give you an indication that it is possible, they don't give you an indication as to whether it is probable.

The probability of you achieving your dream will vary, depending on how much skill you have and how much work you are willing to do.

Take a moment to reflect on your vision and mission. What is it you want to achieve with your life? How would you describe this to people around you? Jot down your initial thoughts on your mission statement, it can be amended later don't worry about having a finished article.

In addition to looking at your vision and mission it is also vital to think about your values.

Below is a list of values with a short summary of what they mean. I want you to choose the six which you consider to be the most important to you. It could be that these are values you are currently living by or aspire to live by.

It does not mean that the others are not important, but I want you to force yourself to reduce them down to the most important six. Jot them down in a pad, if you're reading the paperback version of the book underline them. If you're on ebook, both Kindle and ibooks allow you to annotate a note, so note down the six that are most important to you.

- **Achievement** - reaching or exceeding goals successfully.
- **Loyalty** - being faithful and true to people.
- **Career Focused** - continual progression in your job is important.
- **Customer Focused** - you're driven to deliver excellent customer satisfaction.
- **Having Fun** - ability to laugh and express humour.
- **Entrepreneurship** - you value being your own boss or owner of the business.
- **Team Player** - you enjoy being part of a team.
- **Competence** - you like to demonstrate your abilities and confidence in your knowledge.
- **Accountability** - you are passionate about taking responsibility and ownership for your actions / outcomes.
- **Respect for Individuals** - you believe people are at their best when being their true self.
- **Consistency** - you can be counted on consistently. You value this trait in others.
- **Adaptable** - you thrive on change and are quick to adapt.
- **Family** - spending quality time with significant people in your life.
- **Honesty** - you value the truth, even if it can be at times painful.
- **Legacy** - you want to make a difference to people's lives and leave something for others to follow.
- **Quality** - accuracy and precision are very important to you.
- **Trust** - you believe is vital in all relationships.
- **Integrity** - having values and sticking to them is really important to you.
- **Learning** - you have a lifelong approach to it. You are

always seeking out the new, questi
in your self-development.
- **Risk Taking** - you have courage to take
regularly go outside your comfort zon
- **Recognition** - you like to give and receive
that people need to be thanked for a jc   ⌄⌄ done.
- **Credibility** - your actions always match your words.
- **Open** - you are open to new ideas, new information. You
always ensure everyone is heard.
- **Fairness** - treating people equally is very important,
making sure everyone has a chance.
- **Creative Thinking** - you love new ways of thinking, new
ideas, especially the bold and crazy kind.
- **Commitment** - you are tenacious and will do whatever it
takes to achieve a goal.
- **Passionate** - you get excited an emotional about goals
and aspirations.
- **Urgency** - you value efficiency and people acting with
urgency. You like fast paced environments.
- **Perspective** - you maintain balance in life and work, you
are level headed.
- **Empowerment** - you like to give it to others and accept it
for yourself.
- **Diversity** - you like different cultures, people, identities
- **Being Weird** - you enjoy being different, you like to stand
out and express yourself. You love originality.

Take a moment to consider why you chose those six. Why are they the most important to you? Do you feel they are values you display now or want to display in the future? Would others use these to describe you without being prompted? For example: one of my values is being weird, and yes, people do use this to describe me without the need for prompting!

an aside, I appreciate that some people have a negative association with the word weird, which personally I think should change. Ultimately weird describes different and original, which I value highly.

Now, the difficult part. I want you to highlight the two values which are the most important to you out of those six. Again, I emphasise that the other values are still important, but I want you to mark the two that are the most important.

Think of it as the two values that you could never, would never, compromise.

It is important to be clear on this.

As you undertake your journey for personal transformation it is vital to understand what you will change, but also what you will keep. Your values are what will get you through the difficult times, and your values are what you need to remind yourself of when you are looking for that quick win, that "fix" to a problem.

If along the way to achieving a goal you go against the values that are really important to you then you will create a sense of un-ease, that left unchecked will lead to feeling un-fulfilled, out of touch with yourself and lacking a sense of purpose and meaning.

It will lead you back to where you started.

The reason some people achieve huge success and then realise that they are still not happy is that they have been willing to sacrifice their values, they have been willing to achieve success "no matter what the cost".

This might feel it could work for some, but if the cost is what you value the most, then winning can feel very much the same as losing.

The cost of achieving your dreams cannot be sacrificing what you value the most. Because when you compromise on your most important values, you stop being you.

Let me give you a couple of personal examples.

I was about 12 years old, walking to school in the rain. Alone.

My older brother, on the other hand, was not walking to school. He had demonstrated a certain reluctance to attend school regularly – i.e. he rarely did.

So, in what I believe was an attempt to provide him with positive associations, the local social services team arranged for him to be chauffeured to school in a large Mercedes car. Coming from a family who didn't have any car at all, this technique was offered in the hope it would persuade him to change his ways and break the cycle of his truancy.

However, as I *did* go to school, this opportunity wasn't offered to me. I wasn't allowed in the car. I would set off to school on foot and see the car pass me. My brother waving and laughing in the passenger seat.

I wanted to be in the car. I'd never been in a Mercedes and I wanted in.

I remember one morning, prickling with anger, picking up a loose brick from the side of the pavement and setting my sights on a car parked a few feet from where I stood. Unattended. No passengers.

The weight of the brick in my rain-soaked hand invested me with a visceral sense of power. A choice. An opportunity.

There was no-one around. *If* I threw the brick I wouldn't *hurt* anyone.

Throwing the brick would mean I was a 'bad kid' and maybe then I would get the opportunity to travel to school in a Mercedes like my brother.

I caught sight of my rain-soaked reflection in the car's window and I knew I had to stay true to my values. I might achieve my goal of getting into the car if I threw the brick — but I didn't want to be that kind of kid.

I set the brick down where I'd found it and continued my walk to school.

From time to time we all get faced with what I call the 'brick choice', those moments where you can choose to get what you want immediately, but at the expense of values that you would otherwise hold and defend dearly. 'Smash and grab' without a thought for the consequences.

But then what? Where do you go next if you abandon your values for short term goals?

If you've spent any time in the UK in recent years you will probably be aware of the scandals that have gripped the financial services industry relating to the historic mis-selling of payment protection insurance (PPI) by many providers. In the wake of these revelations many banks have had to refund billions of pounds of PPI premiums to their customers.

I offer this information because, about 13 years ago, I managed the personal loans department for a UK bank. And I can say with absolute certainty that my team did not miss-sell PPI.

I can be sure of this because it nearly cost me my job.

I was insistent that the choice to take PPI always rested with the customer and then only if eligibility had been thoroughly established and the policy fully explained. With hindsight, that all seems pretty reasonable doesn't it? Bizarrely, this was not a common practice amongst many providers in the industry at that time.

As a result of staying true to my values, my department didn't hit the PPI sales target set by the company's senior management team. In fact, compared to the UK average my teams weren't even selling half the PPI sold by other banks and lenders. This led to some very challenging conversations, particularly with the senior executives who had set the targets. I was under immense pressure to hit those targets, *no matter what*.

I could have done what some of my peers in other banks were doing. I could have instructed my team to sell the insurance to customers without them knowing. I could have used the under-hand techniques that I knew others were using, in order to secure a bonus.

But for me this was a classic 'brick choice' scenario. To hit my target and receive the associated remuneration would have meant me going against values that I am very passionate about: customer centricity, ethical selling and customer choice.

So I worked with my team and convinced them of the value in not 'throwing the brick'. We didn't miss-sell the PPI. But I literally put my job on the line in the process.

Of course, viewing the situation in the wake of the PPI miss-selling scandal I feel totally vindicated. I know I made the right choice, but at the time it was tough – I was putting my income and my job at risk. I held my nerve and focused on my values.

Situations like this are testing. But the more you make choices that reinforce your personal values, the more your personal power grows. It is this power base that will get you through the tough times, especially at work.

Have faith in your values; know that they will ultimately lead you down the right path.

Sometimes it won't be easy, and you may have to make some sacrifices. It might mean flying in the face of perceived wisdom or accepted practices. It might mean having difficult conversations. It might be tough, but in the long term it will be even tougher if you wind up looking at yourself in the mirror with the knowledge that you abandoned your values to get you where you are.

If you find yourself facing a 'brick choice', my hope is that you will have the courage to put the 'brick' down and continue on your journey. Even if it means walking alone for a while.

Incidentally, I recalled my childhood 'brick choice' recently when travelling to Bratislava for work. I was met at the airport by the driver tasked with transporting me to my hotel.

The car was a large Mercedes.

Dreams can sometimes come true in ways we don't quite expect.

Let's move on and dig a bit deeper into what your dreams really mean to you.

Have faith in your values; know that they will ultimately lead you down the right path.

Chapter Three – the three Rs...

Reflect:

What are your values? How important are they to you? What is your vision and mission (remember this can and will develop and evolve over time). When have you found yourself in a position that your values have been challenged? How have did you respond?

Respond:

How can you get people to know about your values, your vision and mission, without telling them directly? Take an action to talk to people about them indirectly, i.e. talk about what is important to you without saying to someone "this is my vision". Remind yourself every day what your vision, values and mission are.

Result:

The aim is to get the people closest to you to be able to identify your values, vision and mission without you telling them directly (doesn't have to be exact wording). If it is something you are living by, then others will know. If they don't, then go back to the top and start again until they do.

chapter
FOUR

Dream
Digging

Take a moment to visualise a tree, visualise whatever type of tree you wish, for me it will be an English Oak. Imagine this tree, in a field, on the top of a hill, in a forest, wherever your mind takes you. Think about its trunk, the branches, the twigs, the leaves, hear the wind gentle rustle through them. This tree, no matter how old, how grand, how large and impressive it may be, started out as a tiny seed.

A little bit like your dreams.

Inside your head, your dreams are nothing more than a tiny seed, they need to be nurtured to grow into something bigger. To start the process we will look at something I call Dream Digging. We have to dig into your dream, to get to the root. It is like the tree you are imagining, all the life comes from the root, you can cut a tree down completely, but if you don't kill the root, it will grow back. It will be a different shape, but still the same type of tree.

This is important to remember when we start digging into your dreams. Most of the time when we consider our dreams we visualise the end result, which is great as holding onto this vision helps. However, the end result is not the full picture, in the same way that when you look at a tree you can't see the root system beneath the ground that gave birth to the tree and sustains it, providing it with water, nutrients and keeping the tree grounded during a storm.

The reason we need to do some Dream Digging, is to explore the root of your dream. Why it is so important to you? What it means to you? And what you will do if the dream takes a different shape than the one you had imagined?

This is really important, because just like trees, our dreams can sometimes get knocked down, they can take damage, they may appear as though they have died.

With a real tree, it can sometimes be beneficial to cut back some branches, to re-shape it, to lose some of it. We know it will grow back, in a different shape, but it will grow back.

It is really hard when you have to cut back on some of your dreams, especially hard if you are only focused on what you feel the end dream will look like. We can become obsessed with how we have visualised our dreams, they take on a particular perfection. It can be about how our body will look, of a bank balance we'd like to see, of a career or job aspiration (often down to what type of office you may have).

It's not wrong to want these things, but as they can often take different shapes, or change over time, it can be disheartening to see them not quite as you had imagined.

This is why we must dig into the root of your dream and not just the shape it takes when it's fully grown.

Consider this example, someone who has a dream of going to Oxford University and they are declined. There is no appeal, the dream is over. Oxford University, however, is merely the visible part of the dream, the tree above the ground.

What is the root of this dream? Is going to Oxford a sign of significant academic achievement? To themselves? To others? Is it because they have aspirations of a particular job that they feel would be aided by a degree at Oxford? Does going to Oxford represent a badge of honour and boost personal pride?

There are many things Oxford could represent and many things above that are true, it will help with job prospects etc. However, if the dream is dramatically cut down and crashes to the floor like a felled tree, then it's important to tend to the root system if you want to re-grow the dream.

If you chop down a tree (please don't unless it's absolutely necessary), it will grow back. It will look entirely different, but it will be the same type of tree. It could even be better. Several years ago a young tree at the side of my house was kicked down by some youths, presumably in an attempt to alleviate their boredom, it was sad. The tree has since grown back and it now much bigger and stronger than the one before, though it doesn't look like the same tree.

If you become too focused on only the visible part of your dream, what it looks like externally, then you will pay no attention to the root, and it is the root that will hold the dream in place, and allow you to re-grow it in a different shape if the dream gets knocked down or is forced to take a different shape.

Focusing on only the visible part of the dream can lead to a life of chasing things that never really make you happy.

There are so many examples of people who put so much energy into pursing a particular car, a house, a bank balance, a job title, and when they have achieved it, they feel hollow and empty.

There is always a better car, a bigger house, more money, another promotion etc. But it never really satisfies them, they are never really happy, because they haven't considered why they really want it in the first place, what is the root? What emotional need are they trying to satisfy?

And let me be absolutely clear, there is nothing intrinsically wrong with aspiring for a bigger car, better house, more money and a promotion. Dreaming of financial freedom to do some of these things is not a bad thing in itself, the point is that there is often a lot more beneath the surface of our dreams.

Take my dream of a Plaza apartment in NYC, whilst I've given myself a specific goal I know that it may flex, it may change. The root of my dream is the desire to become more than what I am, an ability to have a home in Manhattan is one representation of that, but not the only one. What I am focused on is becoming more, wanting more, aspiring to be better than I am today. In reality I know I can achieve this wherever I am, it doesn't have to be the Plaza, but if I can make that happen as part of the dream then it's a bonus.

It doesn't mean giving up on your dreams, but recognising that they can take different shapes, and won't necessarily always turn out as you want or expect them. This allows you to be in a constant state of growth, to continue to aspire to become more.

It helps build emotional resilience to get you through the times when the dreams take a turn for the worst, when it looks like they are never going to happen.

When you fail.

Because that is reality. Things don't go to plan, dreams feel as though they've been shattered, more so when you only focus on the visible part of the dream.

Part of the root of your dream is not only why you want it, but what you are willing to sacrifice in order to get it. This is why we looked at values in the last chapter, because if you start compromising on what is really important, your values, you will create an internal conflict that can become a negative and destructive force in your life.

So let's start digging. This is a simple but very effective process that you may have done before. It is called the five, (or as many as it takes) whys.

Simply state your dream and then ask why? Take that answer and ask why again and repeat. Don't stop before four or five and maybe don't go beyond seven.

This process helps you understand what is behind the dream, what is the root? What is it you are really trying to achieve?

You must be completely honest with yourself when completing this exercise, and don't worry if it takes more time than you would expect. It is easy sometimes to simply state 'because I want it' in response to the question, which is the reason you ask why again (you can't repeat the same answer).

Equally the process can lead you down a dead end. Many years ago I did this process with wanting to be a writer, and the why quickly took me down a dead end that I had a dream of being an amazing wealthy writer (very few actually are), and my dream was about financial freedom not writing. Going through the process again, and again, I actually got to the bottom of why I wanted to be a writer, the root of my dream.

I wanted to write because I felt like I had something to say, and I wanted to get it out, even if I was the only one reading it.

If you struggle to go through the process it could be an indication as to why you are struggling to achieve your dream, perhaps you haven't considered enough about the reason you want it in the first place. There is always more to the dream than just the dream itself.

Dream Digging helps you realise that the dream could be closer to you than you realise.

Take for example owning the dream house. Google 'dream houses' and you will get some amazing pictures, have a look at them. It is easy to get drawn into those pictures, to imagine what it would be like to live in some of those amazing houses.

But you will also notice that the pictures of these houses are all missing the most important thing, people. They are missing the most important part of a house, sitting down as a family to dinner, the party where you laughed so hard but can't remember why, coming down stairs on a holiday morning, hearing the winter rain (if you have any) against the window whilst you're warm and cosy inside.

You can look at an empty house and imagine yourself inside it (hence why they don't show any other people), but the dream then becomes about the house and not what you would do inside it. What would you want to do? What would owning that dream house mean? What do you do in your current house?

A dream house isn't about the size of the living room, but the size of the living you do in that room.

A dream car isn't about how comfortable it makes the journey, but how comfortable you are with the journey you're making, there isn't really any point in being comfortable driving to a job you hate.

A dream house isn't about the size of the living room, but the size of the living you do in that room.

What is the point in seeing a bank balance grow as your life shrinks? Money in the bank may give you a sense of reassurance, but money has no intrinsic value, it has to be exchanged for something else to realise its value.

OK, an important point about money. Obviously we live in a world that requires money in exchange for basic life supporting activities such as food and shelter, and it has been proven that too little money can have severe detrimental impact on the quality of people's lives. We all need enough to survive, and a little bit on top. Equally it has been proven that beyond a certain point, money has no impact on the quality of your life.

Around 2014 I read an article about the 72nd richest man in the world, he was desperately unhappy because he felt that he should be in the top 10 richest people in the world. He literally has more than 7 billion other human beings not as rich as he is, but he is unhappy as there are people who have more.

I know many people who dream of winning the lottery, but don't stop to consider what they would do if they did? What is it that the financial freedom of winning the lottery would allow them to do with their lives? When I ask them and do a bit of Dream Digging they quickly discover that they can start doing what they would do now. Probably on a smaller scale, and it will take more time and effort, but stand a bigger chance of becoming reality.

If it is simple financial freedom they desire, again this can be achieved with a greater chance of becoming reality than the odds that are offered on a lottery ticket.

The probability of becoming a millionaire through work are far greater than winning on the lottery.

It will take longer, and it will have a different shape. Ultimately when people dream of a lottery win it is because they believe it will enable them to do things that they feel they can't do at the moment, however there are many of those things that don't require millions of pounds and can be started today.

OK, so sometimes they do cost millions of pounds, such as my apartment at the Plaza.

But I'm not buying a lottery ticket to make it happen.

What do you want and why do you want it? You must Dream Dig before you can move on, or you may find that you achieve the dream, but it doesn't feel how you thought it would. Here's a very personal example:

I, like many people in the world, like many people reading this book, want to lose weight. Back in 2002 I did lose weight, a significant amount, around 70 pounds (nearly 5 stones), I was literally transformed. I was desperate to lose weight, as I was desperately unhappy with how my body looked. I hated my body, I hated me.

But a strange thing happened, I had achieved a massive physical transformation, but still felt the same. I hadn't realised that the way I felt about myself was resulting in my weight gain. I made the mistake of believing that if I changed something on the outside the inside feelings would automatically fall in line and everything would be OK.

It wasn't.

And the weight, and some more, went back on. It has been a long journey for me personally to realise that the body image was just the visual part of my dream and not the root.

I still have weight to lose, sometimes achieving some dreams can be harder than others, it depends on what barriers are getting in the way (I will talk more about those in the next section). Being happier with myself is helping me lose weight. It's about being happy now, not happy when.

Worse than not achieving a dream at all, is achieving the dream and still being unhappy, realising that you feel exactly the same as you did before. Realising that you hadn't become more.

An important part of Dream Digging is realising that you must be happy now, that the dream isn't going to bring you a sense of happiness that currently evades you. An external change will not bring about a permanent internal feeling of happiness.

To give your dreams the best chance, be happy now, not happy when. Be happy with your body now for example, primarily because it's the only one you've got and you need to it to achieve all your dreams.

If you dream of a better job then you must be happy with the one you have now, because at the moment it is supporting you financially (if you don't need the money and are not happy then quit!)

It is vital to focus on being happy now, rather than when, because being happy gives you the best chance of getting to the root of your dream and achieving it. In the next section we will look at doing more in order to become more, and a key element of being happy is that you are more productive, more creative and more adaptive.

Smile. Have fun. Enjoy being you. Now.

As you dig into the roots of your dreams, if you believe that they will make you happy and that you are not happy now then dig into why you feel unhappy. What is the root? How can you address some of those issues now?

If you postpone happiness, in the belief that it will materialise upon the achievement of a particular goal or dream, then I fear you will be forever postponing happiness.

It doesn't mean it's easy, and happiness isn't achieved with a snap of the fingers, but during the Dream Digging process it's important to understand what is driving the desire to become more. Being happy in your pursuit, enjoying the activity that is required to achieve your dreams gives you the best opportunity. As we will explore in the doing more section, if you don't enjoy what it takes to achieve your dreams, then perhaps you don't really want them in the first place.

SMILE.
HAVE FUN.
ENJOY YOU.
NOW.

Chapter Four – the three Rs...

Reflect:

What is the root of your dream? Keep practicing the five (or more) why's to really get beneath the surface. Why do you want what you want? How happy are you about achieving your dream? How can you increase that happiness?

Respond:

What are the different shapes your dream could take? What are all the potential outcomes that would be aligned with the root of your dream? Whilst there may be an ideal outcome, what is second, third and fourth best? Would you be happy with those compared to nothing?

Result:

By digging into the root of your dream you should be more confident that it is achievable, especially given the variety of shapes it may take. Put a note in your diary for a month's time, see how positive you feel about your dream, if you don't then it might be time to re-assess whether you really want it.

chapter
FIVE

Do
More

It is time to act, time to do, time to take that leap of faith.

Time to own time.

There are many reasons why you can't do more, at the top of most people's list is not having enough time.

Well here is a reality check, you will never, ever get more time. It is not physically possible to get more time than you already have.

Without getting into a debate about the physics of time, we can safely assume that it is constant and from a human perspective, it is finite.

Time is not the issue, what you do with it is.

To start with it is important to understand what you are doing with your time, and who is managing your agenda.

When you wake up on a morning I want you to ask yourself these two questions:

What am I going to do today?
Will that be aligned to my goals and dreams?

Now, be prepared. Whilst these are simple questions to ask, the answers may not come so easily.

If you struggle to respond to these questions or are not happy with the answers, that's a pretty strong indicator that there is a disconnect between your goals and your daily agenda.

TIME IS NOT THE ISSUE.

THE ISSUE IS WHAT YOU DO WITH

YOUR TIME.

So what is on your agenda? What are you going to do today? List it all.

You may find that the things you care about most, the activities that are most aligned with your goals and dreams, come near the bottom of your list of priorities. The top of the list tends to fill up with the demands placed on us by other people.

Our agendas tend to get hijacked by other people's priorities. Our phones, emails and social media feeds are all filled with the agendas of others. So, with the finite resources available to us, how do we take control of our daily actions to ensure we can give our personal agendas the time and attention that they require?

We all have the right to pursue happiness and to live the life we want to live.

But we often put our goals on hold because we feel they are at odds with the other agendas in our lives. We have a case of 'agenda clash'. We find ourselves at an impasse – if we're going to move forward towards our dreams then we need to start making some choices.

Whose agenda are we going to follow?

This process may not be easy, because what you will need to do is weigh up the pros and cons of prioritising various agendas against each other. It will mean taking a long, hard look at the activities and priorities in your life.

The process of prioritising may not be an easy exercise to undertake – it takes focus to peer into the future and visualise our goals and dreams from our current position. Furthermore, it takes courage to prioritise our life and agendas accordingly. But this process should help you understand if the agendas in your life are capable of co-existing, or if you feel some are mutually exclusive.

This is important work. Until you have resolved the clash of agendas in your life, gained clarity and insight in to your priorities, you are unlikely to be able to be a success in any of your pursuits – regardless of the agenda you try to follow.

Let me explain: if you continue to work on other people's agendas at the expense of your own, you will need to accept that over time you will develop a sense of resentment towards that activity. It doesn't matter if it's a job or a relationship or some other commitment – if you feel as though the time spent on it gets in the way of your own agenda, you will come to resent it.

But your resentment won't just prevent you from functioning fully in accordance with the other person's agenda. Over time, it will also start to infect the enthusiasm you have for your own goals and dreams.

So, as with so many aspects of personal growth, it comes down to making choices. Potentially difficult choices. But you have the power and the right to make those choices.

You will need to make choices to maximise every opportunity to pursue the various agendas in your life. You have to look at which agendas could potentially be in conflict and make a choice between them. This isn't an easy choice.

Often when we feel we can't commit to our goals because we "don't have the time", we are really choosing to use the time for something else.

It can be that you've had a tough day at work and want to unwind with a glass of wine rather than do the exercise to lose the weight you want to lose. It can be that your mind is so frazzled at the end of the day that you simply don't have the mental capacity to put your mind to moving your dreams forward.

But the reality is that you are making a choice.

If you are choosing to become more then you must choose the activity.

You must make active choices and not passive habits.

This is one of the hardest parts of becoming more, taking ownership for what you do with your time.

The following phrases have to be pushed from your mind, "I don't have time", "I just can't find the time", "There aren't enough hours in the day".

It is important that the language you speak reflects your intention. These phrases are making excuses, they feel valid, but they are excuses.

And the real tragedy is hearing these phrases used when people refer to the things they truly want in their lives – when it relates to their goals and dreams.

Let's face it, as we push to get more and more productive with our lives and with our work it can be difficult to 'find' the time for the things that truly are important to us.

This makes achieving a goal quite difficult. Often other priorities will take over and before you know it your goals are suffering a severe case of neglect. I'm no different. I've had many goals that have required me to re-start the clock.

Nonetheless, it's really important to take control of your time if you are trying to pursue your goals and dreams whilst holding down a 'day job'. However, you may have more time available to you than you realise.

If you sleep for the recommended 8 hours a day, and work a 40 hour week then you have 72 hours left at your disposal over the course of the week. Think about that for a moment. That adds up to 3722 hours every year, or 156 days!

I know I have had times in the past when I felt like my time at work was at the expense of my own personal goals and aspirations. I was working about 40 hours a week on average, often more. But I would have had to work 57 hours a week before I had less time outside work than at my desk. And even then, the time leftover is still sufficient to make gains in the pursuit of your dreams.

I call this time outside of work (when you're not sleeping) 'Out Of Work Waking Hours', or OOWWH. I like to pronounce this as "Ooooh Waaah"

Yes there are many things that pull on our time, and if you have a family and a busy schedule outside of work it can be tough to find the time. Really tough!

But find the time you must. And once found, use it wisely. Do as much as you can with your OOWWH; the more you do, the more in control of your time you will feel. You will start to 'own time'.

It feels powerful and energizing to use your time to work on your goals and dreams. It's a great reminder of the endless possibilities that you have available to you outside your day job.

Owning time also means accepting responsibility for how we use it. When we say 'I don't have time' for something, what that really means is 'I don't want to do it' or 'I choose not to do it'. This might seem a little harsh. Believe me it's not a comfortable thing to say out loud – imagine telling your boss you've 'chosen' to not do that report!

However, taking ownership for our time forces us to take accountability for our actions, which in turn is a crucial step in moving towards your goals and dreams.

You're not going to be given any more time. You have all the time you will ever have.

So make choices about what you spend your time doing. Make choices to do what you want to do with your OOWWH. Inspire those around you to do the same.

Own it. Use it. Be accountable for it.

This is the first step in owning time, changing how you perceive it. If you perceive it as something you have no control over and it is impossible to "find the time" then no amount of "time management" techniques or hints and tips on how to organise your life are going to help.

Own it

Use it

Be accountable
for it

You will be forever a slave to the idea that you don't have time, and other people's agendas will come above your own goals and dreams.

That's why it is important to become conscious of how you feel about time. Become aware when you use the phrases that reinforce a belief in your mind that you "don't have time". When you hear yourself say it you can begin to re-shape your mind-set. Re-shaping how you feel about time, how you respond to the demands placed on your time, how you think about time will enable you to take ownership of it.

The second thing to do is understand how you are currently using your time. There are different ways of going about this, I've personally found the most effective way is to buy an application for your smartphone. There are many versions, search the app store on your phone for Timesheet or Hours Tracker and you should get several options available.

Personally, I recommend spending a couple of pounds or dollars buying the full version of the application, it is a very small investment to make in helping you achieve your goals. The reason I go for the paid version (most of them offer free versions) is that you get to set the activities and make them specific to the tasks you spend your time doing.

The great thing about these applications is to use them as a time card, you are effectively punching in and out of all your tasks. It may seem a little laborious at first, but if you have set your categories accurately you should be able to record everything you do throughout the day. I recommend doing this for at least two weeks if you can, to get as much data about how you are using your time as possible.

You must be honest with yourself, I say this because when you start analysing your time you realise how much of it you do have, or how much of your time you may spend doing something that isn't aligned to your goals and dreams at all.

The hardest part is taking ownership for it, which requires you to be completely honest.

(The alternative to using an application on your phone is to have pad and pen and jot down everything you do throughout the day, but I think the phone app is far more effective and efficient.)

Once you have your data, take a look at it. How much time did you spend on activities that are not helping you achieve your dreams?

Which activities do you want to change? Which activities do you want to stop altogether?

I love the news, you could describe me as a news junkie. I'm not an avid TV watcher, but I would gravitate to turning the news on the TV every day, every morning, and every evening. I didn't realise, until I analysed my time, just how much time I was spending watching the news.

So I stopped.

I still catch the headlines online, but it is far more efficient, I have literally freed up several hours of time each week. Several hours that can be spent on more productive tasks.

Here's another really tough part about owning time, you can't blame anyone else.

Yes, other people impact your time and your agenda, but only if you let them. It is still your life to live, they're your dreams, your goals, if you spend your time blaming the failure to achieve them on someone else then you will never achieve them.

I've accepted with my own personal transformation that the reason I wasn't achieving some of my dreams was because of me, not because of anyone else; and certainly not because of time.

I had to accept that I was just dreaming, and that without doing something it would remain just a dream, forever out of reach.

I realised that I was enjoying the distractions too much. Let's face it, relaxing with a nice glass of wine and good food can feel nicer than going to the gym. Getting engrossed in an amazing piece of television and binge watching the series can feel great.

And distractions are not necessarily bad things, they are things that feel wonderful, that help you relax, unwind and have fun.

And it is important, no vital, to have fun.

But I realised that I was using all my time on distractions, whilst feeling increasingly frustrated that I wasn't achieving my goals and dreams. One of them was to be a writer.

But I didn't write. I would dream about writing, and that dream would usually involve a JK Rowling like success that would enable me to purchase my Plaza apartment. To use the metaphor from Dream Digging, I had dreamt of a huge tree, that grew money! When I did some digging into the roots I realised that I wasn't dreaming of becoming a writer at all, and that maybe I didn't want to do it.

Because I didn't write.

So I started writing. I wasn't writing in the hope of making a billion dollars, I was writing because I wanted to write. Because I needed to. Because it became an important activity, it's priority on my agenda increased.

And now, the actual process of writing is something I love, I enjoy. This is an important lesson I learned.

You must enjoy the activity it takes to achieve your dream, or you will be setting yourself up to fail. Now, failing is natural and I will discuss more of that in the next chapter, but for now, think about the activity you know you need to do in order to achieve your dreams.

If it's losing weight, do you enjoy managing what you eat and exercise? If you don't enjoy it, if you feel that with managing your diet you are denying yourself, if you feel that the exercise is a punishment for being overweight, then you will struggle to lose weight.

If you want to be an actor, do you act every day? Even if you are alone, facing a mirror and practicing an emotion or an accent, reading some Shakespeare etc.

Whatever it is you want, do you enjoy the activity to achieve it?

Don't get me wrong, I get how it feels "in reality". In reality you feel as though you have no time and what little time you do have left you are so emotionally exhausted by living your life that you can't find the energy to start doing something more than what you are currently doing – no matter how much you may enjoy it.

So let's start out small, and think about how we get the energy to do more.

All action starts with a single thought, an idea, and I'm sure you're familiar with the image of a lightbulb hovering over someone's head when they have an idea.

Think about that reality, the lightbulb.

A light bulb hovers over the head of an inspired individual, signalling that they've had an idea – *a bright idea* – a eureka moment.

How much energy is there in an idea? In a thought? How much energy do you have to expend to get the great ideas?

The average human brain consumes about 300 calories a day, an average of 12.5 calories an hour.

If we convert the calories required for a single thought into electrical energy we would find that an actual 'light-bulb' would barely register a flicker. A thought doesn't cost us a lot of energy but they contain immense power. The power to change the world, to change people's lives. To change your life.

Many of us lead very busy lives and the pace of life seems to be forever increasing. Getting to do what you want to do can be hard. Finding the time, and the energy to do things is tough.

Summing up the energy to exercise after a long day at work can be difficult. It can be challenging to work on the house, play with the kids, cook a meal rather than order in. Plus all those jobs that seem to be mounting up…

It's really, really hard.

When it comes to your thoughts however, you don't need to find the energy, you have it already.

Every action begins with a thought. Transforming your life, becoming something more than you are today, achieving your dreams – it all starts with a thought.

Your thoughts have the power to up-lift you, to support you, to enable you to change the world around you. They also have immense destructive power, they can hold you back, they can stop you rather than start you, they can convince you that you don't have the energy, or the time to live the life you really want.

It comes down to choice. Your choice.

So be conscious, be mindful of your thoughts, be aware of them. Harness their power for good. Determine how you want to put that energy to use.

Release all that immense potential into your life. Not tomorrow. Not after you've 'rested'.

Do it now. Pick one small thing that you can do that will move you towards your dream.

I encourage it to be as small as possible, so small that you cannot give yourself the excuse of not doing it.

I know it's a cliché but every person who climbed Everest started out by making one step at the base of the mountain.

What is your one step? What is the one small thing you can do right now? Put down this book and do it.

Make a commitment to do it again tomorrow, and the day after that and the day after that. Make it so basic and simple that you cannot give yourself any excuses, no matter how tired you are, no matter how mentally drained you are. Prove to yourself that you can do more.

Don't worry about how small it is, all our successes in life can be broken down into individual steps. Your heart will beat approximately 1 billion times in your life, think about that, it would actually take you longer to count to a billion than the time it would take your heart to beat to a billion! One single heart beat compared to a billion seems insignificant, yet each and every one of them is as important as the other.

Every beat of your heart, every breath, every blink of an eye. It is your body, constantly in a state of motion, constantly doing more each day.

You can do more than you believe you are capable of.

Don't concern yourself too much at this stage with how long it will take you to achieve your dream. Depending on what you dream is the time it will take to realise it will vary, it could be longer than what you realise, it could be shorter. I would always encourage you not to be disappointed if it takes longer than you want.

You can do more than you believe you are capable of.

Be open to choosing the long journey, don't expect too many quick wins so quickly. I've been there myself, I've made that mistake, of wanting to see weight loss happen more dramatically, of wanting to finish writing a book in a week, finish a painting in a day, learn a language in a month...

Some people do achieve these things, which makes us all want the same fast quick progress and there are many people and companies out there promising you fast progress towards whatever you want in your life. I make no such promise.

I'm not saying quick progress isn't possible, you may be surprised once you start doing more how quickly you can progress. I know that once I actually started writing my first book on the Sales Conversation it happened much more quickly than I had initially anticipated, this book has taken significantly longer.

The point is that it may take longer, be open to that possibility and it makes whatever action you choose more sustainable.

We all have within us a need for instant gratification, we want the short cuts, we want the results now.

Be mindful of this desire because it may take you a longer than you realise, but it all starts with the first small step. Once you get into the habit of doing more, a little bit each day, you will notice that you can do more than you realised.

You will allocate the time, the energy, the effort, because you will start to see progress.

And a really amazing thing about the way we humans perceive time, the more you do with your time the more time you feel you have.

The secret to getting more time, is do more with your time.

Dedicate just 30 minutes a day to doing more, activity that supports your dream. That is just 2% of your day, (OK 3% if you minus your 8 hours sleeping).

That is the start of doing more, just 2% of your day, you can spend the other 98% doing whatever it is you do, all I am asking for right now is that you devote 2%.

You protect that 2%, you make it a priority, no matter what.

If you can't, if putting aside 2% of your time is impossible then I challenge you on whether you really want the dream. What if the dream became reality and it occupied all of your time? How would you cope with that if you can't even allocate 2% to it?

Devote 2% of your time and enjoy it so much that you push it to 4%, to 8%, so

that the activity occupies your time, so that it becomes your time.

You want to achieve your dreams? Great – do it.

Of course, no matter how hard we try, sometimes we fail, which I will cover in the next chapter.

Chapter Five – the three Rs...

Reflect:

How do you feel about the time you have? What do you do with your OOWWH? Are you happy with how much you get done in the time you have?

Respond:

Complete the time diary! Whether it's with the help of an app on your phone or pen and paper, I urge you to complete the time diary. Be honest. Try, if possible, to pick a typical couple of weeks (no point in completing it whilst you're on holiday!)

Result:

How much time do you have? How much time are you spending on things that are not adding any value to your goals? How much time are you spending doing something that is actively working against what you want to achieve? The minimum amount of time you are looking to allocate to your goals and dreams is 30 minutes, ideally 1 hour each day.

chapter
SIX

Failing

At some point, something is bound to go wrong, some activity will not produce the result you want, things will not turn out as you had planned them.

You will fail.

Not in life, not at everything. Some of these failures will be small, some will be so big you can't imagine how you will recover. Some will be anticipated, others will catch you completely by surprise.

Sometimes bad stuff happens. We're cruising along feeling pretty good about the progress we are making, and then we get blind-sided by some unfortunate event. Illness, bereavement or a financial set-back.

Problems rise-up and knock us down. We're scared and vulnerable, as we face our mortality and the fragility of our circumstances. We're reminded that the plans we have spent years constructing can collapse in the blink of an eye.

We feel pain, confusion and we want to vent our discontent. We want to rally against that which hurts us.

We jump to apportion blame and absolve ourselves of responsibility for the hand we have been dealt:

'But I'm a good person…'
'Why me?'
'What did I do to deserve this?'

The anger and indignation we instinctively feel give us an emotional crutch to lean on. They provide a sense of stability and control. We hold onto these feelings. Some never manage to let them go.

But the support we gain from our anger and indignation does not last. In reality, these feelings immobilise us; while we expend energy fighting against the injustice of our circumstances, we miss the opportunities to learn, to forgive and, most importantly, to move on.

Every situation presents us with a choice. Pure and simple. We can choose how we react to any given situation, no matter how challenging it is. We can choose how people, situations and our circumstances affect us.

As the old saying goes, "Pain is inevitable but suffering is optional".

Make no mistake – this is tough to accept and even tougher to implement. But taking ownership over our responses when we face difficult and distressing times will set us apart from so many others who never recover from the punches life has thrown them.

We will all experience pain in some form at some time. It is inevitable.

Whether we view these experiences as obstacles or opportunities is up to us.

That doesn't make it easy, especially if some of those failures come in the form of rejections.

Rejection: noun – refusal, spurning, dismissal, elimination, to throw back, declining, turning down, no…

However we define the word we all know the feeling, and it's not pleasant. No matter how good someone is at wrapping it up and emphasising the positive, being rejected is tough.

But if you want to achieve success, in any part of your life, then you must get used to rejection.

Quite simply, the most successful people in the world have had the most number of rejections. The best sales people have the highest number of rejections – because they make the most offers; the best entrepreneurs create more ideas that never get beyond rejection in order to create the one idea that takes them forward.

You have to recognise that rejection is part of the process – learn from it if you can – and keep going.

Of course it can feel personal – I felt that acutely when I had a script rejected by the BBC several years ago. It was my work. At the time it felt like they were rejecting part of me. It feels personal, for example, if you're an actor and you get rejected after an audition. It feels personal if you get turned down for that promotion you've been working on for the last two years. It feels personal when you've worked on a proposal and the customer decides to go with a competitor instead.

Rejection feels personal. It can hurt.

But the only way to avoid the discomfort of rejection, is to never put yourself in a position where you can receive it.

Don't send in the script...

Don't audition for the part...

Don't apply for the promotion...

But the main problem with this approach is that you're actually rejecting yourself, and that's the worst form of rejection *and* the most personal...

When you reject the ideas in your head before you explore the possibilities that lie within them....

When you see yourself as not good enough to send in the script...

When you see yourself as not worthy of the promotion...

If you want to transform your life – if you want to live the life that is truly fulfilling to you and your family, a life that allows you to fulfil your true potential – then you have to take risks. You must be willing to be occasionally uncomfortable.

You have to be willing to face rejection.

The more you put yourself in a position to receive a rejection the closer you will be to achieving your goals.

The feelings we have surrounding failure are learnt, and we have a strange way of dealing with failure as an adult.

We accept that failing is part of learning in children, when they are learning to walk we accept that they will wobble and fall. When they learn to talk we accept that they will make noises that eventually turn into words, often those words will be wrong. But we don't chastise those failures, we recognise them as part of the learning process.

Entirely different once we reach adulthood. If, like me, you've ever attempted to learn a foreign language as an adult, the most difficult part is the fear of failure. I learned Spanish enough to understand a great many words and conversations, but found myself unable to form a sentence when anyone asked me to say something in Spanish.

The fear of getting it wrong, the fear of failing, overwhelmed me so much that I couldn't get out a single word. Despite knowing that failure was part of learning, it still stopped me.

The fear of failing is very powerful.

And yet it is a natural part of the learning process, when you fail at pronouncing a word in Spanish you can always give it another go.

Sometimes with our goals and dreams we experience failures from which there is there is no coming back. You fail an exam at school, there are only so many times you can do a resit, before you are told you have failed. That failure could lead to a failure to get a place in the college you wanted, a failure to get into the university you were desperate to go to, a failure to secure the job you wanted…

Failure can go on.

But like many things in our life, how we deal with failure is down to a combination of our circumstances and our response to those circumstances.

Sometimes our perceived failures could be a result of actions we took previously, not as a direct result of actions we are taking now.

I remember several years ago when I felt like I had failed.

The fear of failing is very powerful.

It was 6:45am. I was cold. And it was raining. Hard.

The kind of heavy, grey rainfall that seems to soak you to the core. I was standing at the bus stop, as I did most mornings at that point in my life, waiting to catch a bus that would take me to a train that would eventually lead me to my desk at 8:30am.

Not only did I feel wet, I felt indignant. I was a senior manager, standing in the rain, whilst many of my colleagues drove themselves to work in the comfort of their luxury cars. As the rain beat down, I started to feel upset and angry that I was standing in the rain and not travelling to work in the warmth and comfort of a luxury car.

Make no mistake it was a proper pity party, with just one person on the guest-list – me.

But then it dawned on me – I realised that I had chosen to be there. I had made certain choices in the past that meant I couldn't afford a nice car at that moment in my life.

I had made choices that meant I would stand in the rain on that morning, waiting for a bus.

Taking responsibility for our choices is much harder than we often realise, especially when it comes to the things that are important to us. On first consideration, this might seem strange – surely the things that are most important to us naturally lead to us taking more responsibility?

But I've often found it can be the other way round.

Taking responsibility for our well-being, our finances, our relationships – the list goes on.

The reason taking responsibility can be so hard is that it forces us into a situation where we have to make decisions, and these decisions have to be made in 'real time'.

What do I mean by 'real time' decisions? Real time decisions are the ones we make every single day, in every moment. Our situation, our feelings, our goals, our outputs and our future are a culmination of 'real time' decisions – the decisions we are making every day in the moment of 'right now'.

As a result wherever, and however, we find ourselves right now – career, health, body shape, financial situation – is a reflection of choices made. I have chosen to be in my current situation. You have chosen to be in your situation.

As a senior manager I felt like I had failed because I didn't have the nice car, I didn't have the artefacts that would identify the success I thought I'd achieved.

In fact I felt the opposite of success, I felt like a failure.

It was difficult, but I remember having a moment of understanding, when I realised that I had created the situation I was in by decisions I had made previously. I was the reason for my perceived failure.

Taking responsibility for our failures can be tough.

It requires us to check if each decision or action, including our previous actions and decisions, are aligned with our goals. We all have some goals that seem harder to achieve than others.

As I stood contemplating on that cold, rainy morning, the realisation that I could take responsibility for my choices it changed my mood and my outlook forever. Whilst it was still raining I was suddenly happier. I actually remember smiling to myself.

I wasn't regretting my past choices – I'd already done and achieved things that I never imagined I would. I was happy to still have those memories and would not re-write my decisions.

It was previous decisions, to do things in my life that meant financially I wasn't in a position to have the luxury car. If not having a particular car meant I had failed, then I had created that failure by my previous actions.

At that moment I realised the immense power that exists in accepting and taking responsibility for my actions and choices. In so doing, I was able to start taking responsibility for my decisions every day and face a future free from regrets.

Naturally, this doesn't mean I always make the right choices. There are still a lot of things I'm working on. But it does mean that I feel responsible for myself and have no blame, anger or frustration with others for my own circumstances.

Take responsibility.

Feel the power you have to impact your own life, your dreams and your purpose. Take responsibility for the 'real time' choices you make today, tomorrow and every day and I promise that you will reap the benefits.

Taking responsibility for your failures requires you to reflect and understand what type of failure it has been. You could group failure into two main categories, to keep it simple let's just call them good and bad.

Good failure is when you have tried your best, you've put in all the effort you could have, there is nothing more you could have done and you still failed.

That happens, it's life. You reflect, you learn, you move on.

Bad failure is when you could have done more, you know you didn't really try hard enough, you know you didn't put in all your effort. You failed because you didn't want it bad enough to make it happen.

That happens, it's life. You reflect, you learn, you move on, *and* you make a decision about what you will choose to regret about your future failures.

When you fail at something you are ultimately going to have a regret in some form, so it's important to consider regret as part of your plan on how to deal with failure.

Regret is to feel sad, repentant, or disappointed over something you have done or failed to do.

However it's defined, we're all familiar with regret. That horrible sinking feeling of disappointment, of failure. Those thoughts and moments when you wish you could turn back time and do something all over again.

Perhaps it's a wish to make different choices... undo the bad decisions... say something differently... avoid the wrong turns.

But of course we can't do that. We have to live with our choices. Which, I guess, makes regret a pretty pointless emotion. After all you can't undo things, un-say things, or go back and take a different turning in your life. And even if you could, you have no idea whether that would have led to a better outcome.

It's easy to look back and think 'if only', but you then allow your imagination to play out a different set of circumstances that seem brilliantly better than the situation you're in today.

But it is just that – imagination. It's not a different path your life could have taken, because it doesn't exist.

So that's it – regret solved. Sorted. Worry no more!

Ah, if it were only that simple...

Besides, regret isn't all bad. Whilst it might be nice to have the attitude 'I regret nothing', the reality is that sometimes we should regret. It is an important way to remind ourselves that we are human. That we are still learning, that we are still making mistakes. A dose of reflection, a bit of regret, can help embed that learning.

Our choices exist only in the present moment; whilst we can't go back and undo things we regret, perhaps we can be a little more proactive when it comes to choosing how we think about regret.

Our regrets can fall into one of three categories:

– Will
– Might
– Won't

You **will** regret some things, such as staying up late partying when you have an early start or important meeting the next day – you **will** regret it in the morning. But understand that, and be mindful of the fact that you can make a choice: accept that in the morning you will certainly regret it, or do something differently.

You **might** regret some things, such as eating dessert if you are trying to lose weight. One dessert isn't necessarily going to impact your goals... but if you miss your weight target at the end of the week, you **might** regret it. Your choices **might** lead to unforeseen circumstances, but if you are comfortable with this then you can be more efficient in your decisions.

Then there are those actions that you know you **won't** regret. I've mentioned previously my ongoing goal to lose weight. Whilst I'm not keen on exercising I realised the other day that I have never regretted exercising. Once it's over, I know I **won't** regret putting that time aside to focus on me and my goals. It's an activity that I find is really and completely regret free.

So, when thinking about the decisions we have, the choices we make on a regular basis, it's important to consider what type of regret might come with those choices. It doesn't mean we won't make mistakes or live without regrets. But it does allow us the opportunity to undo some of those choices before they've been made.

Will you regret it for sure? Perhaps you might? Or do you know with certainty that you won't regret it?

It's not about living a perfect life. Sometimes regrets can make great stories. They can provide fun and amusing twists and turns in the narratives of our lives, even if they come with unwanted consequences.

Focus on being mindful of the opportunities that are open to you. Enjoy the fact you have a choice.

It's up to you. It always has been and always will be.

Whenever you fail you will have some form of regret, by reflecting and understanding that form of regret helps you shape and change how you will respond in the future, and what choices you make about potential failures.

The key to dealing with failure is learning to develop more patience. Having more patience to try again and again, to learn from each failure and to keep going.

Perhaps you're looking for instant success, maybe you're looking for the tide to turn on just one wave. I had this thought on a recent trip to the coast.

I love the sea. I love the smell of the sea. I love how the sea looks. I think that, most of all, I love the sound of the sea. I love the sound of the waves crashing against the shore.

Of course when you look at a single wave it's almost impossible to tell whether the tide is coming in or going out.

Tides don't turn in one single wave.

It takes time to determine whether it's coming in or going out; you must be patient. You must wait and watch the sea for a longer period of time than it takes for one single wave to crash against the shore. It takes time before you can confidently turn to the person next to you and say, "Ah-ha, I was right all along! The tide is coming in! No, wait... maybe it's going out!"

You have to "wait and see".

Tides don't turn on a single wave.

It can be difficult having the patience to "wait and see" when it comes to our personal transformations.

What you may perceive as failure could just be part of the process, it may take more attempts to achieve a particular goal over another.

Whatever your dreams are, whatever your personal challenge, remember that each day you make a choice, which is aligned to your goal, it will bring you closer to making it happen.

You can have the healthy mind and body that you want. You can have the dreams you want. You can have the car, the house, the success, the career – whatever it is you want, you can have it.

Just don't expect it to come in on a single, almighty giant wave; those types of waves tend to destroy dreams, not fulfil them.

And it is possible to be failing at one dream whilst being successful with another. It is vital that you don't let the feeling of failing at one goal infect all your goals and dreams.

There are many goals and dreams that I have realised in my own life so far, when I stop and consider the amazing journey I've been on since I was 13, I have literally achieved so many of the dreams I've had.

It could be said that I am literally "living the dream".

There are, however, others that still evade me. Other goals and dreams where I have failed, and continue to fail. It has taken me a long time to realise that I had let failure of some goals infect how I felt about others.

I was allowing myself to feel like a failure, by focusing on the goals I've still not achieved. It distracted me from feeling fabulous about all that I had achieved.

Success won't come all at once, and there will still be aspects of your life where you experience failure. Some goals and dreams you have may take significant amount of time and effort and you will continue to experience failure.

It doesn't have to stop you from becoming more.

But it can.

Embrace the failure as an opportunity, it could be that the failure itself may lead to an unexpected success. Perhaps you can turn a bad situation into a brilliant one?

We all have bad days, weeks and months. Some people have a bad year. Whilst our reactions to our circumstances can have a huge impact on how we feel, there's no denying that sometimes those failures hit us hard, sometimes we are dealt a bad hand.

Sometimes circumstances seem so bad that they consume individuals; perhaps it seems that there are situations that cannot be turned around.

That said, I want to tell you a story of a small boy in France called Louis who was born in January 1809. Like most children, Louis was curious about the world, and one day whilst exploring in his father's workshop (his father was a leatherer) he hurt one of his eyes on a tool used for punching holes in the leather.

Unfortunately Louis' eye became infected and very soon the infection spread to his other eye. Tragically, it wasn't long before Louis was completely blind.

But Louis and his parents were determined that they would not be held back by the new circumstances and challenges that they faced. Louis attended school and performed brilliantly, helped by a new system that was being used to help visually-impaired people read. The system had been originally used to help soldiers read instructions at night time and was based around a series of embossed dots and dashes.

Whilst this reading system helped Louis greatly, over time he found it lacking – a system designed to deliver short specific orders to soldiers wasn't capable of capturing the rich nuances in the language of a Shakespearian sonnet; it wasn't a complete substitute for the written word.

Louis decided that his circumstances would not hold him back – he wanted more. So he developed a new system, one I'm sure you're familiar with as it's the system that is still used throughout the entire world to help visually impaired people read. Louis' surname was Braille and the system he invented bears his name to this day.

What I find most amazing about Louis' story is that the instrument he used to emboss the surface of the paper with the small dots that form the Braille alphabet was the very same instrument that had caused his blindness some years earlier.

What an incredible example of taking a situation from bad to brilliant.

Life can sometimes feel unfair. Things can happen to us that cause us to slip, trip, stumble and fall. Occasionally those falls can be big ones... so big we wonder if we can recover.

But, like Louis, we all have a choice about what we do next. Louis didn't accept that his circumstances should limit his opportunities; when he experienced barriers and obstacles he worked to remove and overcome them.

Louis continued to battle an education system that was reluctant to use his new invention; in his lifetime the Braille system was never utilised – it was two years after his death when Braille became adopted as standard. But a couple of hundred years later and Louis' legacy lives on throughout the world.

Not all of us will have the opportunity to leave such a far-reaching legacy. But, if we continue to reject the notion that our circumstances define us, if we continue to want more for our goals, our dreams, our lives... we all have the capacity to change the world. We're all capable of doing so.

Think of Louis – if he could transform his situation from bad to brilliant, why not you?

You wouldn't use Champagne to celebrate a failure would you, but you may be surprised to learn that Champagne itself was a form of failure. Dom Perignon, the monk who originally created Champagne accidently put the wine through a second fermentation, giving the Champagne it's lovely characteristic bubbles.

Dom Perignon spent many years trying to get rid of "those dam bubbles", as he perceived them as a failure.

Viagra was initially designed as a blood pressure pill, during testing it was discovered to have an interesting side effect on male patients.

Champagne and Viagra (I'm not advocating a combination of them both!) are examples of failures turning into multi-billion dollar industries.

Embrace your failures, you never know, some of them might end up being your biggest success.

Chapter Six – the three Rs...

Reflect:

What have been your biggest failures in your life to date? How did you overcome them? If you've not yet overcome them, how are you going to? What parts of your life still feel like a failure? Are you letting them infect your whole life, making you feel like a failure?

Respond:

Remind yourself daily that you are not a failure. You are an amazing person, with unlimited potential. Commit to use the three regret categories for all your choices, Will, Might, Won't.

Result:

How did making decisions using the regret categories help you make choices more aligned with your goals? If they didn't, try again, and again, and again. Don't give up.

chapter
SEVEN

Habits

We form habits, habits help us learn, they help us live. Habits become routine, they allows us to navigate our day without allocating too much of our cognitive resources (our mind) to mundane tasks.

Without habits our minds would be overrun with making hundreds of decisions each and every day.

Habits help our minds because they are passive, they don't require us to pay too much attention to them, we can keep our attention for more important matters.

To become more it will be necessary to become aware of your habits, and which ones could be unwittingly working against you achieving your goals.

Passive habits will often lead you to the easiest course of action, but easy may not be what you want. Most people find it easier (and often more fun) to gain weight than to lose it.

It's easier to keep the TV on the in the background than turn it off and do something more productive.

It is easy to let your life drift by, as though you are just a passenger in your own life.

To become more it will be necessary to become aware of your habits, and which ones could be unwittingly working against you achieving your goals.

The hardest part of the "easy" is that over time your frustration grows, when you feel distant from living the life you want. When this happens it becomes easier to blame the failure on someone else rather than take responsibility.

This blame can become a habit, in fact I call it a virus, The Blamè Virus. I first noticed the Blamè Virus (pronounced "blah-may") when I began a coaching job, about seventeen years ago. I call it a virus because it infects us and once we have it we can easily infect others. Generally the virus is at its peak when things are going wrong but once you get it there is a danger it could seep through to all aspects of your life. It becomes a habit.

You'll have probably had a bout of the Blamé yourself at some point in your life. You'll certainly know someone who has it. There are multiple symptoms, but here are some common ways in which it manifests itself...

Individuals "blamé" their poor health on not having the time to exercise or eat healthily; individuals "blamé" their failure to gain a promotion on their boss or colleagues; individuals "blamé" their inability to achieve their goals and dreams on their parents, family or friends; individuals "blamé" a lack of money for the fact that they're not enjoying life.

Of course all these things can have an impact on our lives and our work. External factors do influence our lives and sometimes prevent us from doing things. But here's the problem: at its worst some people really believe The Blamé Virus is responsible for *every* misfortune in their lives. For some it becomes the only answer – their only excuse. Some people become long-term carriers of the "blamé" and don't realise that they have absolved themselves of any responsibility for their lives or any possible actions they could take to own and resolve a problem.

It can become a passive habit to blame other people, other things, other circumstances, this habit is easier than making an active choice and take ownership.

The only known cure for the The Blamé Virus is to start developing a mindful awareness of it, to start listening to yourself and others and spot the symptoms of The Blamé whenever, and wherever, it arises. When you become aware of the excuses, both within yourself and from others, you realise that you have a choice. You can continue to allow The Blamé Virus to infect you, or you can choose to drop it. You can challenge others around you to make their own choices. The more that you make conscious choices the stronger your immunity to the virus will be.

The real danger with The Blamé is that years of your life can drift by without you feeling in control of it, without you realising your full potential. Even if others around you continue to be infected, you *can* choose differently.

So what are you going to do? Continue to allow bad habits to get in the way of you living the life you want?

It's not going to be easy. The thing about habits is that they are comfortable, they generally feel nice and most of the time tend to fit in well with others. Like it or not but human beings are herd animals and we all tend to move in the same direction of our 'herd' (work colleagues, friends, community, country) and as such making active choices rather than passive habits can be hard.

Humans are formed, develop and move within highly structured groups. Individually, we are hardwired to coordinate and align our behaviours with those in our herd.

And although we like to think we make our own choices, have our own likes and dislikes, the vast majority of these conform on some level with the group we are in. Research has shown that the fear of social disapproval can trigger the brain's 'danger circuits'. On the other hand, the act of conforming can have a calming and soothing effect.

There is comfort in knowing that your choice is the same as others – making the same choices as the rest of the herd provides us with a sense of reassurance. It offers validation. Similarly, if the herd collectively takes a 'wrong-turn', we can take comfort in the fact that we won't be lost on our own.

"We'll all be in it together, for better or worse!"

This neural programming makes it difficult for us to make a choice that goes against the herd. If an individual's behaviours differ from the majority, the group will notice and often question them. You can witness this dynamic play out in the most familiar of social settings. For example, if you're the only one in the bar not having a beer people will often encourage you to indulge…

"Go on! One little drink won't hurt!"

Or perhaps you decide not to have a dessert at the end of the meal…

"You can't skip dessert – I'm having one and I'll feel guilty if you don't have one too!"

It can happen with clothes and fashion – if you wear something that no one else is wearing you might stick out. People may even laugh at you – to your face, behind your back or through social media shaming.

The TV programmes we watch, the sports teams we support, the music we listen to, even the food we eat – they're all varying degrees of pressure to conform with the rest of the herd are everywhere.

Moving in your own direction. Swimming against the current. Dancing to your own beat. However you want to phrase it, doing something different can be tough and challenging.

Changing your habits doesn't just impact you, but for those around you as well. The actions of a non-conformist send ripples through the rest of the herd.

Moving in your own direction.

Swimming against the current.

Dancing to your own beat.

However you want to phrase it, doing something different can be tough and challenging.

Some find it uncomfortable because it makes them question their own behaviours.

To be a non-conformist means becoming comfortable with the fact that other people will be uncomfortable.

So why do it? Why go it alone?

Choosing a different direction, can lead you to vistas filled with new opportunities. Forging your own path will enable your mind to function more creatively and identify alternative solutions to the problems or challenges you face in your life and work.

Furthermore, it also feels great to know that you might inspire someone else to do the same thing. That one person who draws strength from seeing someone charting their own course might, in time, start taking their own tentative steps in their own unique direction...

The great thing about it being your life, is that you get to do what you want with it!

So be brave, be bold, and be willing to go it alone if you have to. Have the courage to stand out from the crowd.

Live life on your own terms.

Break free from the herd. Make an active choice rather than a passive habit.

The great thing about it being your life, is that you get to do what you want with it!

Reminding yourself that you have a choice can be the really hard part.

"We always have choice. We say we have no choice to comfort ourselves with a decision we've already made..."
J. Michael Straczynski 'Babylon 5'.

I loved these lines when I first heard them. They clearly articulated the ownership we all have with our choices, and reminded me never to use that awful phrase "I have no choice' – regardless of whether I'm using it to excuse present or past choices I've made.

But, strangely, accepting that you always have a choice can feel liberating and limiting at the same time...

It can liberate your mind when you accept that you always have choice, that nothing is final, that you are in control of your own life. It feels great to keep – and know that - your options are open.

However, it can also feel limiting when you realise you must accept that everything is your choice, especially how you choose to react to things that happen to you. You know the times: when things are not going particularly well, when the world seems against you, when there doesn't seem to be any options.

When this happens it becomes increasingly easier to find the external reasons for your current predicament. "I have/had no choice" absolves you of responsibility and transfers the 'blame' for your life, situation and emotions to other people, objects and events in your life.

You might tell yourself that the job restricts your choices, that the mood of your boss determines whether you have a good day at work, or that the mortgage and the bills determine what type of job you feel you can 'choose' to do.

The danger is that when you convince yourself that what happens to you is completely beyond your control, you become a passenger in your own life and your actions will be led more by passive habits than active choices.

Sometimes it will be tough, sometimes it will be easy. But at all times you are free to make a choice.

How you choose to exercise that freedom... well, that's up to you.

One of the things that will help is becoming more aware of the language you use and ensure it accurately reflects your intention. Previously I mentioned how the language you use about time can impact how much time you feel you have.

Eliminating the phrase "I don't have time" is one way of changing your mind-set.

Our use of language, and the words we choose, reflect our thoughts and motivations. That's why it's so important to choose your words with care, to be mindful of the language you use. Becoming conscious of the words you use, and then changing them, is the first step to adjusting your mind-set and taking full ownership for all aspects of your life.

Many years ago I began to eliminate the word "need" from my vocabulary and replaced it with the word "want". The word "need" suggests an external pressure and perhaps a lack of motivation; by changing it to "want" I found I could take full ownership for whatever it is I'm aiming to achieve.

So the phrase "I need to exercise" becomes "I want to exercise". In a work setting the phrase "I need to achieve my targets" becomes "I want to achieve my targets". The phrase "I need to spend more time with my family" becomes "I want to spend more time with my family".

This very small change in language can trigger an incredible change in attitude and outcomes.

Of course, it takes time and effort to become fully conscious of all the words you use; you have to literally listen to yourself all the time. I still catch myself occasionally using the word "need" and it provides me with a reminder of how easy it is to slip back into old passive habits.

Taking full ownership for your life, your work, your dreams, is an important step towards living a fulfilled life. Accepting that the results you achieve are a direct result of you and your actions can be tough sometimes, which is why it's often easier to talk about what you *need* to do. "Need" has a way of distancing you from the action, as though it's nothing to do with you.

To choose your words carefully is a small, but very important step towards living the life you want to live and turning passive habits into active choices.

Start today. Start now.

Now let me be absolutely clear on something, habits are not bad things. I've probably overstressed it a little in terms of the passive habits being bad compared to active choices.

Habits do help us, as they keep our minds free to concentrate on other things. The point is that you may have habits that you are not aware of (hence why I refer to them as passive) that could be making it far more difficult to achieve your dreams.

This is why I want you to become completely conscious of your habits and choices, so that in time you will create new habits. Habits that will enable you to achieve your goals and dreams, habits that support living the life you want to live.

One of the habits to develop is the habit of showing up for success.

Woody Allen once said that "eighty percent of success is showing up".

There's a simple truth at the heart of his statement: if you show up to an interview, an audition, the gym, you've already got a huge advantage compared to those who didn't show up at all. Also, once you show up – once you're present, evident and committed – it's easier to follow through.

In the same way, it's important to 'show up' for your life if you want any measure of success.

This means showing up regardless of what day of the week it is or what else is going on in the world. It's important to work on stopping random, external factors influencing how we think and behave.

Show up. No matter what.

No matter what day of the week, you are still living your life. If you believe anything is getting in the way of you living your life then you have two choices: either change it or change how you react to it. Whether it's a job or a relationship – if you're feeling miserable, trapped, or stuck in a rut, these are just states of mind and you have choices about how you respond to them.

Stop deferring your life. You don't have to wait until the weekend, next week or next year. You don't even have to wait until tomorrow.

Show up

No matter what

But you know that, don't you?

It is always your time, it is always now. We're all familiar with the sense that there's a lack of time or that time is running out. So please don't waste a minute of it waiting to show up.

Although the notion of 'showing up' is simple, I'm not suggesting it's easy. Sometimes there's real, hard, determined work involved in summoning up the strength, character and resolve to show up.

But remember, if we follow Woody Allen's advice, once we've nailed the 'showing up', there's only a further twenty percent to focus on.

So, please, no more excuses. Be present, evident and committed to living a successful life. Show up today…

Make showing up a habit, make starting today a habit, not waiting until tomorrow or Monday.

You will still have bad days, and you will still have days when you can't be bothered to show up, so don't.

It's your life and don't beat yourself up too much if all you want to do is relax, binge watch the latest Netflix series, drink wine, eat cheese, laugh.

Just be conscious of what is turning into a habit, and whether you're showing up more than you're not.

When you do show up, how do you develop the habit that will enable you to be fully present, how can you develop a habit of making your mind fully available, so that you can focus on maximising whatever time you have.

It is necessary to get into a habit of organising both your mind, and the world around you.

Our minds are only capable of making a certain number of decisions each day. This number can vary depending on the type of decisions you have to make; we all know that some decisions are easier to make than others. Our cognitive resources are limited in their capacity to make decisions; and the more decisions you have to make the less cognitive resources you have available.

If you have several programs open on your computer it uses active memory to keep them running in the background. The more tasks you want your computer to perform, the more slowly and more frustratingly it will operate. Similarly, when our cognitive resources are occupied by lots of decisions, from the small to the large, it's like running a bunch of programs in the background.

Those huge decisions you keep putting off, or the small stuff that gets bumped on to tomorrow's to-do list, all take a toll and leave you emotionally drained, struggling to focus on anything more than passive activities like watching TV or listening to music.

The big problem here is that you need the full capacity of your cognitive resources if you want to achieve your goals and dreams. Sadly that important stuff often gets neglected because our minds are constantly occupied with other decisions and thoughts.

So how do we free up our cognitive resources to focus on the good stuff?

Whilst we can't escape that fact that we will always have decisions to make, we can organise our lives, our homes and our working environments to ensure that many of our decisions have a really low cognitive impact. The simple act of organising your house or office to reduce the frustration of being able to find the things you need or the clothes you are going to wear, will have a significant impact on keeping your mind focused.

This may seem small, and the activity of organising your sock drawer hardly seems like it is going to help with achieving your life dream, but please don't underestimate the value in organising your physical environment.

I personally have been amazed by how easier it is to concentrate and be creative, even after a tough day at work, when my physical space at home is organised.

Then of course we need to deal with those mental "programs" running in the background. Consider what are the big things that seem to be occupying your mind: what are you doing about them? (FYI – just thinking about them or, in the worst case, worrying about them doesn't count!) Once again, it comes down to organising. Invest some time listing all the decisions and concerns that are lurking in the background. Physically write them down in a spreadsheet, in a notebook, on your phone – whatever works best for you – and then detail a plan of action to address each item.

It's about creating a personal environment where you can free up your cognitive resources for whatever you want to achieve with your life.

Organising to minimise cognitive drain will help you create a state of mind that leaves you emotionally charged at the end of the day, buzzing with excitement about what you've achieved and the opportunities that lie ahead.

The reality is that the amount of information we get presented with and the number of decisions this forces upon us is on the increase. So take action now to ensure you free up the capacity of the most valuable resource you've got. Continue to dream more, because you *can* do more and you *will* become more.

So you have habits. That's not a bad thing, your human. You also have choices. Choices lead to habits. Habits either help or hinder the achievement of your goals.

If they're helping, fantastic keep going. If they are hindering, then choose to change. Some habits you may need to change, some you just need to let go.

Chapter Seven - the three Rs...

Reflect:

How do you feel about your habits? What habits do you have that you know are not helping you? What new habits do you need to form to replace them? (don't try to just stop, they are fulfilling a need, how else can you fulfil that need?). How much choice do you truly feel you have?

Respond:

What is your action to change your habits? Make a commitment to become mindful of the choices you are making, when you are making them. It's not about beating yourself up about your choices, it's about recognising that they are choices.

Result:

After being mindful of your choices and eliminating the Blamè Virus for a month, what difference has it made? How much more in control do you feel? What new habits have you formed? Don't worry if it takes you a lot longer than a month to master this, and everyone will still slip and fall from time to time. The trick is not giving up, keep going.

chapter EIGHT

Letting Go

On your personal transformation journey it is important to recognise what you will hold onto and what you will let go of. We can often find ourselves getting this the wrong way round, letting go of our values, our time, the things that really matter, and hanging onto things that don't, such as jobs we dislike, to pay for "stuff" we are worried about losing.

We cling to things that are temporary in their nature, and we need to learn to let go.

Everything in your life, including your life itself, is temporary. Everything is "of the moment". You are the only constant in your life, you are with you for your whole life, however long or short that turns out to be. Everything else, *everyone* else, is transitory.

This is why it's so important to be able to let go.

You must be willing to let anything and everything go because the reality is that, at some point, you might have to: your car, your job, your partner, your salary, your possessions. There are no guarantees.

When you realise that all these things are of the moment, that they are only in your life on a temporary basis, you can truly appreciate them in a more meaningful and satisfying manner. The realisation that you don't have to try and hang on to things as tightly as you did before can be incredibly liberating. You don't have to stress about what possessions you have or worry about your job or status.

172

Letting go isn't about neglecting the things you care about, it's nurturing a supreme gratitude for all the magic those moments bring to your life, however brief they may be.

Perhaps you're having a tough time at work?
It's temporary – let it go.
Perhaps you're going through a difficult time in your relationship?
It's temporary – let it go.

Let go of the things that get in the way: anger, hurt, desperation and worry. Those things can only hold you back.

Life itself is of the moment; temporary and sometimes shorter than we'd like. If you can embrace this, rather than worry about it, you're moving closer to appreciating all the moments in your life that make it breath-taking, dizzying, magnificent and fabulous.

One of the reasons we find it so difficult to let go of the things in life that are temporary is that we are constantly having our expectations shaped as to what we should care about. It takes a lot of effort to break through that noise.

It takes effort to not compare yourself to others.

It can be difficult to get through a single day without comparing yourself to other people.

Advertisers spend billions of dollars trying to get us to buy their products by bombarding us with images of individuals who are generally younger, better looking and, apparently, living a far more exciting life than our own.

How do I compare?

Do I measure up to them?

And then there's the lifestyle-envy we can fall into when we scroll down our news feeds... Recent research carried out by the University of Missouri found that the regular browsing of Facebook can trigger a sense of envy if the user compares themselves to how well their friends are doing in their new job, new relationship, new home.

The report explains that this sense of not measuring up to the achievements of your peers can lead to feelings of depression.

Reality check #1. Not everyone's life is as fabulous as they make it out to be on Facebook!

Yes, it's great to have aspirations. It's great to have goals and dreams. Sometimes it helps to look at others who've achieved their goals and gain inspiration from them – they prove it's possible.

IT TAKES A
LOT OF
EFFORT TO
NOT
COMPARE
YOURSELF TO
OTHERS.

Take inspiration from others, but there has to be a balance.

We all live our individual lives, and everyone has their own stuff that they have to deal with. Sometimes it's easy to look at others and think they have it better, easier, richer...

Look at them – they've got it all 'going on'.

Sometimes it's tempting to look at other people's lives and wish yours was just like it. But if you do that, you take your attention away from your own life, and how much potential and all-round *fabulosity* it contains.

Right now you might be having a bad day, week, month... even a bad year. But, while you're having a bad day because you've not hit your target weight (yet), or achieved that promotion (yet), or realised that dream (yet)... someone could be looking at your life with envy, thinking you have it all.

So what good does it do to compare ourselves to others? Why do so many of us engage with such a negative activity?

It usually stems from a lack of self-worth and self-belief. We use the negative comparisons as a means to justify why we've not yet achieved our goals. We convince ourselves that we aren't young enough, thin enough, good-looking enough or rich enough to make a success of it, that we've not had the breaks or head-starts that the successful have.

We are where we are now because 'we're not them'.

Reality check # 2. "YOU'RE NEVER GOING TO BE THEM!"

It may be a cliché but you're all you've got. You can only be you. I can only be me. You are stuck with you for your whole life. What others are doing doesn't matter because everything else is temporary – the only constant is the self.

The self that is gorgeous, luminous, talented, stunning, epic, flawed, funny, wonderful, generous, beautiful, unique…

In other words, the "self" known as 'You'.

Yes, *YOU!*

We deny ourselves the possibility to be all the above, and more, if we spend all our time envying others. We waste energy and time that we could invest in becoming all we

Surely it's better to be the best version of yourself, than an imitation of someone else?

Let go of how you feel compared to others, you are not living their life, you're living your life. If you don't, then you will give in to envy and jealousy, these are negative emotions that will hinder your ability to live the life you want.

It's fine to take inspiration from others, but if this inspiration becomes a constant comparison it can lead to a negative mind-set, and it creeps in without you realising.

Surely it's better to be the best version of yourself, than an imitation of someone else?

I've been there, I've allowed jealous thoughts to creep in, I've become negative and bitter, feeling that other people were getting a better deal than me. Feeling a sense of unfairness, that I had it worse off. But all it did was hold me back, it was eating away at me, making me feel negative and unhappy.

My feeling wasn't having any impact on the people's lives I was jealous of, it was only impacting me, and not in a good way.

I wanted to let go. I wanted to let go of negative thoughts, because they were only having a negative influence on my life and ability to live it on my terms.

Negative thinking can lead to negative motivation, for example: you want to lose weight because you *hate* your body. You want a new job or promotion because you *hate* your current job or current boss.

Negative thoughts can render our positive actions redundant and our dreams can become ways to reinforce a negative perception that we have of ourselves.

You are highly unlikely to succeed at an interview for a job if the driving force behind you applying is to get out of the job you are in. You must want the job you are applying for more.

You are highly unlikely to succeed in losing weight if you hate your body, as it's your body that is going to have to do the work.

Your mind and body will be far more productive when in a happier state, let go of the negativity, it is no helping, at all.

One significant feeling you will need to let go of, is the feeling of losing. It has a significant impact on how you feel, but more importantly the decisions you make. Let me explain with a familiar example.

Imagine the scene: you're sitting in a chair, heart pounding, trying to make a decision. Do you take the banker's offer of £20,000, or do you play on…?

Many people will be familiar with the gameshow 'Deal or No Deal', in which a contestant randomly opens a series of boxes to reveal amounts of cash, whilst playing 'against' the banker who will periodically make offers of cash to end the game. The desire is to win the big prize of £250,000, hidden in one of the sealed boxes – or to at least walk away with more than the banker has offered them at some point in the game.

But interestingly, the vast majority of people walk away with less money than they got offered from the banker…

Why is this?

What is happening when the contestant has an offer of real cash in front of them, available right there and then, yet they choose to play on? Why are they so afraid to lose a potential pot of cash that they don't yet have?

The powerful psychological force at work in these scenarios is known as 'loss aversion'. Loss aversion was first demonstrated by the psychologists Amos Tversky and Daniel Kahneman and it refers to the human tendency to strongly prefer avoiding losses to acquiring gains. Studies on the subject suggest that, from a psychological perspective, losses are twice as powerful as gains.

Whilst 'Deal or No Deal' breaks down the concept to its most basic form, most game shows are based on this idea.

But loss aversion doesn't just impact behaviours on a game show; it can have a very powerful impact on how we make choices throughout our lives. It can affect all sorts of scenarios – including ones which have far greater consequences than opening a sealed box on national TV.

Some employers offer benefits and bonuses to their workers, betting that they will stick around to receive them, even if they don't like the job very much. People who were very unhappy in their jobs have told me that they can't quit because they're waiting on their bonus. Although they've not actually received the cash yet, the perceived future loss of something weighs more on their minds than the gain of moving on and being happier in a different job.

In the worst scenarios, I've known people stick in a job for years because they didn't want to 'lose' out on a potential redundancy pay out if they were to leave. The perceived loss of a payment they may or may not receive is more attractive than the gain of being happy?

Doesn't that sound crazy?

The same applies for perceived losses of our time. How much time it will take you to achieve your dream.

It takes time, it takes focus, it takes effort. It will mean changing habits and sacrificing some activities, even some relationships, that you may have hitherto enjoyed.

It might mean 'losing' something.

So the challenge is to focus on what you stand to gain, in place of the perceived loss. It takes time to train the mind to focus on the actual 'gain' and away from the perceived 'loss'.

Because our minds can so easily focus on believing we are losing something that we don't actually have, it's important to 're-wire' our thinking and move our attention to what is important and what we actually stand to gain. In doing so we can begin to banish all sorts of anxieties associated with perceived losses, risks and our fears around failure.

Make no mistake, this is tricky, challenging, and potentially life-long work, but it affords us the ability to more readily pursue our dreams, fulfil our potential and live the life we want.

Letting go of what you feel you are going to lose is very difficult, but incredibly liberating. You see many people, especially employers, use loss aversion as a way of getting you to confirm and comply, to accept things that you don't necessarily want to accept. This isn't done maliciously, it is a natural part of how we have come to motivate people to do their work. It isn't necessarily effective, but many businesses don't seem to want to accept that there is a significant divide between how human motivation works, and what they want to do to "motivate" their employees.

Many years ago I left a company a month before the annual bonus was due to be paid. If I'd stayed just another month I would have got my bonus, and it wasn't an insignificant amount of money. My manager at the time couldn't understand why I would give up my bonus, he didn't seem to understand that I wasn't focused on losing my bonus but what I was gaining by joining a new company.

Yes, in the short term I was technically worse off, but I wasn't willing to risk the opportunity that the new job offered by staying in my old one.

The sense of freedom that letting go of the feelings that loss aversion gives us is amazing, but hard. Let's face it, we all need money to function. As I mentioned above, I've known, and still know, people who sit in jobs they hate because they feel they can't do anything else. Or that they are not willing to lose the lifestyle they've become accustomed to.

For me it makes no sense, living an unhappy life to maintain a particular lifestyle. It begs the question what exactly are you living for? The accumulation of "stuff" in our lives is growing at an alarming rate, but if buying the stuff is getting in the way of your happiness, then stop.

Let it go.

As I mentioned at the start of the book, there is nothing wrong with wanting things, there is nothing wrong with aspiring for a bigger house, a better car, particular clothing brands etc. There is nothing wrong in consumption, we live in a world that has an economic system based on consumption.

The point is this, if the things you are consuming and accumulating have turned from being a reward to being a bribe, you must let them go.

What do I mean by a bribe? If your house, your car, your clothes etc are bribing you to stay in a job you hate, then let them go. They are not worth giving up your life. In the scheme of things life is so brief that it isn't worth sacrificing it for things that have no intrinsic meaning.

Are you being held down by a lifestyle you want to maintain?

Consider the ground beneath your feet – is it supporting you, or holding you down?

When you think about it, it's really doing both. You are supported by the ground beneath you, the Earth. But it's also holding you down through the force of gravity.

Jobs can be like that too. They can support you by providing you with an income and paying your bills. They can also hold you down: they can tie you to a particular role, a position, a desk.

We can easily grow accustomed to the support a job gives. Perhaps we also start to believe that they're our only option. After all, to listen to our heart – to follow a calling – well, that's for someone else to do. Someone who doesn't have your life, your commitments, your excuses. We don't want to put the house, the car and the holidays at risk. But are those things supporting you, or holding you down?

How about conversations with family members, significant others and friends? They can have a significant impact. Do their words of counsel seem supportive, or are they holding you down?

It's not about quitting the day job and walking out – I think that would be foolish. But it is about making a choice.

Making a choice to enjoy the day job because it is supporting you. Or, if you feel the job is holding you down, making a choice to work on building a different career path.

Recognise that your actions, your activities, your daily routines, who and what you choose to listen to from your friends and family, are all contributing to where you are right now.

We can choose to view most circumstances as either supporting us or holding us down. Often it's a bit of both. This isn't a bad thing – we're all simultaneously grateful for gravity and the ground beneath our feet.

But, whilst you can't change Earth's ability to hold you down, a lot of what holds down our dreams comes from within, from inside our minds. That's something you can change. It takes work and effort – transforming our ways of thinking and adjusting our perspectives is not a quick job. But it can be done. Little by little, we can choose how we perceive our circumstances.

Because ultimately the question isn't whether a job, a person or a situation is holding you down. The question to ask is this:

"Am *I* supporting me, or am *I* holding me down?"

Are you hanging onto things in a belief that letting them go will hurt you? It's OK to be afraid. Fear is a natural emotion that has served us well over the seventy or so thousand years that we've been around.

But the fear of loss, of the unknown, can hold you down. It can, will and does prevent us from living the life we want. Don't live an unhappy life. If the job is providing you with a lifestyle that you want, but you feel you hate the job, then change how you feel about the job if you really want that lifestyle. Or achieve the lifestyle through another job (a job that you want).

But if like many you dream of more, of doing something more satisfying, of doing something more meaningful, then you will need to let go.

You will need to let go of your fear, the fear of what you may lose, the fear that the dream may not turn out as planned. Ultimately you may need to let go of the dream itself.

What I mean by this is that your dream could have become so perfect in your mind, be so wonderfully brilliant that reality is going to struggle to deliver it. When this happens it is possible to become gripped by fear, a fear that if you pursue a dream and fail, what do you have left?

Dreams in our minds can be so perfect that they sustain us, we can watch them in our minds like a movie with a perfect happy ending; having dreams like this can get us through tough times in life. However, those dreams are fragile, breakable, they need to be protected. They can't be risked.

Letting go of the dream, if it's become unbreakable in your mind may be the way forward. The dream may take a different shape, but if you can't let go of a shape you know will never happen then the dream will only serve as a negative reinforcement of a life you're not enjoying living.

Again, it is important to remind you that I'm not asking you to give up on your dreams, but if you are so specific about your expectations without compromise or ability to accept a variation on your dream then you could unwittingly prevent yourself from ever doing the activity to support it, out of fear that the dream won't be realised as it is in your head.

That's why it may seem a little strange, but the best thing you can do in order to realise your dream, is let it go. Even if just a little.

I still believe that dreams can come true, goals can be achieved, even after years and years of trying and failing. I haven't given up, and neither should you.

Because when it comes to your goals and dreams, when is it your 'last chance'? Have we created a culture of 'last chance'? Why do we buy into the 'last chance' myth?

People in their early twenties take to the stage on TV talent shows and the judges tell them that this really is their 'last chance' to make it into stardom.

The hosts and producers of these shows around the world don't tell the young hopefuls that more people join that chosen profession each year without participating in a talent contest.

And so the insidious myth of 'last chance' pervades.

And what a shame if that's what we believe…

What would have happened if J K Rowling had accepted the first, second, third (and more…) publisher rejections to the first Harry Potter novel? Imagine if she'd believed the 'last chance' myth.

Other myths we're told (and are sometimes inclined to believe) relate to age, body shape, time, energy, money. If we let ourselves get caught up in these deceits we deny ourselves the chance to make a beautiful and distinct contribution to the world. Regardless of what the talent shows say, you have the opportunity.

If you have a story in your head – write.

If you have a song in your heart – sing.

If you have something to offer (and we *all* have something to offer) – give.

Don't engage with the 'last chance' myth.

You have the chance. You have many chances. New chances arrive every day. Just remember that it only becomes your 'last chance' when you give up.

Don't let anyone tell you that your chances are all used up.

Take to the stage – amaze yourself today and every day with how brilliant you truly are.

Letting go isn't about giving up.

Letting go of hate, anger, resentment, fear, and negativity isn't about giving up. These emotions are reinforced on a regular basis, they creep into our minds unannounced. It takes time to clear you mind, it relies on you being conscious of your thoughts and a willingness to let go.

To do this successfully, you may need to pause from time to time, stop occasionally.

We are all on the move. The pace of life seems to be forever increasing. Life is fast, work is busy. Too much to do in too little time.

Our lives are a frenetic ball of activities bouncing from day to week, week to month, month to year. And it doesn't ever seem to stop.

When was the last time you had a moment of pure stillness? A time when you didn't need to be somewhere, do something, speak to someone? When you could just be still? Is it even possible to be truly still?

Don't let anyone tell you that your chances are all used up.

Perhaps stillness doesn't really exist because everything is always moving. We are all on a giant rock hurtling at 66,000 miles per hour through space, and space itself is moving, as well as our galaxy which occupies that space. Our solar system is moving through space at nearly a million miles per hour. If you feel sometimes that you're trying to get somewhere in a hurry, it's nothing compared to our solar system!

Ultimately, stillness is relative to what is happening around you. To be still is about your reaction to what is happening around you, the action and activity you undertake in response to your environment. Whether it's work, family, friends, or just the "stuff" that makes up your life, how you react determines how still you can be.

And being still in this increasingly fast-moving world is becoming more and more vital, essential and precious. It may feel like a luxury for many. Maybe you feel you simply don't have the time to be still; the pressure is too much, the work is mounting, the expectations don't allow. Where would you find the time?!

The life is yours, the time is yours, do with it as you will.

Because when we are still we can listen, reflect, pause, understand, and choose. When we are still we give ourselves opportunity to look at things in a little more detail, to spend a little more time, to realise the potential of the possibilities that are in front of us. Enjoy that whenever and however you can.

It in those moments of stillness when we can let go of the things that are holding us back that we are most open to letting in the things that can help and support us.

Chapter Eight – the three Rs...

Reflect:

Take a moment to look around you, at all your stuff. Does it make you happy? Is your salary a reward, helping you live the life you want, or is it a bribe? Keeping you living an unhappy life, feeling trapped, unable to consider doing anything else? Have your dreams become unbreakable? Are you so afraid of not achieving them that they are preventing you moving at all towards them?

Respond:

Build time into your daily routine to be still, even if only for one minute each day. Take a moment to stop, turn everything off, no distractions. Breathe. Become mindful throughout your day how much fear is controlling your thoughts, fear of losing. By becoming aware of it you are more likely able to challenge your own mind to be better than what it is right now. To ensure you are not unwittingly working against yourself.

Result:

I'll be honest with you...this one, will take time, possibly a very long time. Not comparing ourselves to others when you are being bombarded daily with marketing that does just that, isn't easy. Continued work on letting go should help you feel more positive and less fearful about what you might lose. Focus on what you will gain, not what you might lose.

chapter
NINE

Letting
In

It is important to recognise what you have to let in as well as what you must let go. It is not just about eliminating fear and negative thought; it has to be replaced with a new, more positive internal dialogue.

It is also important to let others into your dreams as well.

For many years I wanted to be a writer, it was my dream from a very early age. I would regularly talk about being a writer, even though I didn't write. Because I had developed a perfect dream in my head and it was so perfect and complete that it was impossible to make it happen.

I wasn't just in fear of failure, I was paralysed by it. Any attempt to make my dream come true would not live up to the amazing movie I was playing in my head, which meant that my dream would be shattered and broken.

I had an unbreakable dream.

On the odd occasion I would do some writing, and the even rarer occasion I would allow someone else to read it, I didn't take feedback very well. Because I didn't write often I wasn't getting the practice I needed to become better, because I sought feedback even less I equally didn't become practiced at listening to that feedback.

Invariably the feedback would point out what I could do better, but I couldn't let that feedback in. My unbreakable dream had me as an amazing writer, feedback on what I could do better didn't align, it challenged the dream, it put it at risk. So it was easier to stop getting feedback, and by not letting that feedback in I was preventing myself from learning and improving.

I was actively blocking myself from achieving my own dream.

How crazy is that? I didn't know it at the time of course. As a result of me not taking feedback well I stopped sharing. I became closed and protective about my ideas, about my dreams. It was safer for them to stay in my head, like a ship in a harbour.

The safest place for a ship is in the harbour. But it's not really what a ship is designed for. It is destined to sail the high seas, no matter what the conditions. Sometimes it will be rough, sometimes it will be an idyllic journey into the fabled sunset.

Your ideas are like ships.

Ideas seem safe if they're cocooned in your head. But that denies them any purpose or value.

Yes, they're safe, but they're also un-tested, un-lived, *un-sailed*.

By contrast, getting the ideas out of your mind's harbour – clearing all moorings, unfurling the sails and pushing off into unknown waters – that feels like a risky business.

What if the idea doesn't work?

What if other people think my idea is silly?

What if I fail?

These concerns are natural, and perfectly understandable. After all, if a ship leaves the harbour and sinks to the bottom of the sea, it's never going to sail again.

But, of course, before a ship sails from the harbour it undergoes many tests to make sure it is sea-worthy.

You can do this with your ideas.

Share your ideas with a small group of trusted people – your closest network of family, friends or colleagues. Explain your idea and get them to ask you questions, to 'stress test' your idea. Ask them to look for holes – we don't want a ship that will start leaking after we set off!

Be willing to really listen to their ideas and feedback – don't get defensive or precious about your idea. If it's an original concept it may be difficult for some people to grasp or understand at first. Be patient – just imagine how weird the initial ideas of flying in aeroplanes, landing a man on the moon or carrying your entire music collection around in your pocket must have sounded when first discussed. I confess that I still struggle to get my head around the very proven concept that a giant 50,000 ton cruise ship manages to float on water!

So take on board the feedback, ideas or suggestions you receive. Modify your idea if you need to, or if you want to. Take the opportunity to add to your idea, to refine it, to look at it in new ways.

Then set sail.

Get your idea out there, however you can. Share it. Enlist advocates – after all, a ship needs a crew! Create a buzz. Do what you have to, what you *want* to. Just keep sailing.

Yes it is risky, and the reality is you may fail. Your ship may sink. The ocean floor is littered with ship wrecks, from many years of brave sea-faring. But we have learned, and can continue to learn from each ship that sank. But, thankfully, failures at that level are now exceptionally rare.

If your ship sinks – swim to shore. Learn from the experience. Then build a better ship and set sail again.

Whatever you do, don't leave your ideas in your head – a ship that stays in the harbour will never take you anywhere.

Which is a shame, because there's so much ocean to explore.

The more you let feedback in, the more you let others into your dreams the more chances you are giving of making your dream come true.

Whatever you do, don't leave your ideas in your head – a ship that stays in the harbour will never take you anywhere.

All your friends and family want you to succeed, want you to live the life you want, sometimes they may not understand it, sometimes they may be so fearful of failure on your behalf that they want to protect you from disappointment.

But the more you let them in, the more you give them a chance of feeling about your dream the way you do.

As well as letting in the feedback, you are letting in the chance to learn, grow and become better at what you love. Equally you are letting in the very real possibility that you can win, that you will succeed. This is vital because the fear of failure can run deep.

Our minds are very good at enlisting a whole battery of emotions to work against us, such as fear, embarrassment, negativity, etc, the mind does this in the belief that it is trying to protect us from harm.

Let in the possibility that you will succeed, let in the potential that you have. One random day whilst getting something out of a kitchen drawer I was reminded about the amazing potential of all life, and its ability to strive for more. It was a cupboard potato.

Cupboard potato?! Surely I must mean couch potato. That's the phrase most people are familiar with. Generally used in reference to a person who sits lazily, motionless on the couch. As if they were a potato.

I don't like the phrase; I think it's unfair to potatoes.

You see, potatoes never just 'sit there'. It might look like they do, but they are in constant motion. Once out of the ground, with no access to water or nutrients from the soil, they are in a race against time. It may look like they are doing nothing, but that couldn't be further from the truth.

When I was rummaging through the kitchen drawer, in search of something, I felt something unexpected, something unfamiliar, brush against my hand. A little shocked by the sensation, I withdrew my hand quickly. Clearly, my mind reasoned, there was some rare breed of man-eating spider in the drawer.

However, upon further investigation I found that it was something entirely different. It was a pale tendril, a sprout from some plant or other. It was huge...

Having carefully followed it back to its source, I discovered it stemmed from a very small potato which had clearly fallen down the back of the kitchen cupboard some time before. Shrivelled and on its "last legs", this small, tiny, apparently motionless potato had produced a sapling over two metres in length. It was quite amazing.

Despite being well out of its 'comfort zone', despite finding itself in an almost impossible position, despite being the poster boy for 'lazy', this tiny potato was in search of the light.

This cupboard potato didn't consider for one minute where it was. It didn't consider the 'reality' of its situation. It didn't question whether it could achieve its goals, or face the fear of failure. It did none of these. It's just a potato after all.

But it kept moving. It kept growing. It pushed and searched for life, because that is what life does. It sought to maximise its potential, to grow into something more. Something bigger, something better.

We are all in a race against time, and sometimes we find ourselves stuck in places we don't want to be. Sometimes the reality of our situations makes our dreams and goals seem impossible, and let's be honest, sometimes they are.

But regardless of our circumstances, regardless of our fears, regardless of 'reality', there's one thing we could all learn from the cupboard potato: don't stop.

When you think about it – what other choice do you have?

Let in the possibility, let in the chance, let in the excitement that you have potential to become so much more than you are right now.

Let in the feedback to help you get there. Let in the challenge, the questions, the uncomfortable conversations that might break the dream. Let in the ability to adapt and change, to re-write and re-shape your vision as you make it reality.

I want you to think of your favourite film. Now think of your favourite scene in that film. The dialogue, the imagery, the performance. Think about how much you love it; how much it means to you. Think about how much you consider it to be perfectly brilliant.

Chances are it didn't start out that way. That scene could have gone through numerous re-writes before it became the perfectly brilliant version you love.

But you don't get to see the re-writes.

Our goals in life, whatever they are, have to go through 're-writes'. But, all too often, we want the finished product straight away. We're impatient to see the 'perfectly brilliant' version. Going through many iterations, experiencing the process of creating and making our goals and dreams come to life can be very difficult.

The re-writes challenge us.

If you're losing weight it's easy to step on the scales and experience, for the most part, constant disappointment that you haven't got to the finished goal. If you are wanting to change your career, or achieve happiness at work, it is difficult to go through the process of making that happen. It could take a lot of 're-writes' before you get where you want to be.

During the 're-writing' process we must adapt our goals, we have to change our plans, our expectations. We learn that things are not as easy as we want them to be. Perhaps not as easy as we feel we deserve them to be.

Sometimes things will go in the wrong direction. Sometimes we fail. Getting back up to do it all over can be hard. But it's in the re-writes that things get better, during the process of learning, re-creating, changing and adapting. The wonderful process of making things better.

So whatever it is you want to do with your life, realise that the process to achieve it will require many re-writes, and that's not a bad thing.

Embrace the opportunity to adapt and learn. And if you're not happy with any aspect of your life, start your re-write today.

Let it in.

I no longer tell people I'm a writer, instead I write. Telling people was a mask, a smokescreen, to keep people away from my unbreakable dream I had in my mind.

I let people in, I broke the dream and I've never been happier or more positive about where I am right now and the potential of where I am going.

Let it in, live the life you want, become more.

Embrace the opportunity to adapt and learn. And if you're not happy with any aspect of your life, start your re-write today.

Chapter Nine – the three Rs...

Reflect:

Are you letting in the people you care about the most? How many people are aware of your dreams? Of what you really want with your life? Are you willing to go through the rewrites with your goals and dreams, to keep working on them, refining them, learning and growing?

Respond:

If you've not done so already, start letting people in on your goals and dreams. Start enlisting advocates, you may be surprised by just how many people want you to succeed. Consciously focus on letting in the positive rather than the negative.

Result:

It will quickly become clear which of the people you let in are pushing you forward, and which are holding you back. Keep you time and energy focused on those which are pushing your forward.

chapter
TEN

Becoming More

What does it mean to become more? Will it happen with a fanfare and an award? Probably not. Becoming more is something that will constantly evolve, it will become part of who you are and what you want.

It will shape how you see the world, how you respond and react to the circumstances you find yourself in, how you use the precious time you have, to live the life you want.

Don't worry if you still feel as though you have unanswered questions, it isn't about having all the answers, besides, answers can be boring.

When you have the answer you no longer have the question. The journey of discovery has come to an end. The party's over.

As human beings we have innately curious minds, and have been asking questions for thousands of years. And for thousands of years we have found "answers" that were later found to not be answers at all.

So if it's a choice between the answer or the question – I'll take the question every time.

Answers are final and represent the end of the search – a passive and comfortable place to rest. Questions keep driving us forward in an active, sometimes uncomfortable, search for more. Questions are the very essence of curiosity and, for me, there is nothing more exciting than curiosity. Curiosity represents growth and development.

A child's incessant "why? why? why?" reveals a mind continually absorbing, assessing and wondering. The child's mind exists in a perpetual state of curiosity – always active. Like a muscle, the mind becomes stronger the more active it is. Questions and curiosity make our minds strong and agile.

The act of questioning engages the mind in an active search for new ideas. As such, the curious mind remains open to fresh possibilities and anticipates the arrival of new ideas. When they appear, new ideas are more readily identified and embraced.

It takes questioning and curiosity to dig beneath "normality" to find hidden treasures. Life remains an adventure.

That's why I'll keep questioning, keep being curious and keep being excited by not having the answer.

It used to frighten me that I didn't know things, "knowledge is power", a phrase I'm sure you've heard, maybe you believe it. The problem with holding onto knowledge power is that it is quickly becoming irrelevant; you know something and someone else can quickly "Google it" and know just as much.

I'm now more excited by what I don't know, because the unanswered questions represent potential for more, for the journey for the journey to continue. I have become more than what I was before.

Of course becoming more isn't a finished state, I'm not perfect, and I'm glad that I'm not, being perfect would be having all the answers, how dull would that be.

Becoming more is remaining open.

Think about how we see doors in either one of two states – open or closed.

It cannot be open when it is closed and it is not closed when it is open.

What about our minds? What does it mean to be truly 'open-minded' or 'closed-minded'?

I consider myself to be open-minded, but was recently challenged (and rightly so) when I expressed cynicism towards a particular learning technique. The fact that I was challenged on my cynical, closed-minded response, gave me a bit of a mental-jolt and I was able to re-consider my perspective and be more receptive to the topic being discussed.

Sometimes we view our minds and the opinions that develop from them as being solid, immovable, unchanging. If we encounter someone whose views strongly oppose our own, we might perceive them as

BECOMING
MORE IS
REMAINING
OPEN.

'closed minded' and mark them with that label for life. We might decide that is who they are, and always will be – forever entrenched in a particular mind-set. Always stuck in that way of thinking.

Meanwhile, of course, the closed-minded person doesn't tend to see themselves that way. In fact they will often see things the other way around, casting themselves as open-minded and you as the opposite. They've just formed a view and are sure of their opinion. Nothing wrong with that. It is good to have a sense that you are sure of your opinion and that you are certain of what you are talking about.

So... could the belief that you are an open-minded person be just another variation of the 'closed-minded' person's certainty? Are they two sides of the same coin..? Two sides of the same door..?!

Without an open mind we couldn't learn about the world around us, about ourselves, our relationships, our potential. Open or 'closed' minded, we have all learned our responses, behaviours and beliefs at some point in our lives.

Does true open-mindedness exist? Could it be that all minds are open, but some are more open than others? I guess that a door can be left 'ajar' – not quite open, not quite closed. In that state, depending on your perspective, it might appear to be open *or* closed.

Perhaps we all maintain various states of 'ajar-mindedness'.

The great thing about a door being ajar is that it only takes a tiny push to open it a bit more. Wider... and wider... and wider.

Try giving the door of your mind a little push further open and see what happens.

Be prepared to see a little more of what's outside and invite a little more inside.

Be curious about what might be on the other side.

Be curious about what *you* might be on the other side...

You never know what you might be missing out on.

Becoming more is maintaining an active curiosity about yourself, the world around you, the potential. Never accepting the status quo, challenging yourself and others to be better versions of themselves.

But as I mentioned previously, this won't always happen with a fanfare, better versions of ourselves happen in small incremental steps. You will have flashes of success, and perhaps you will get a fanfare and an award, but remember that's just a moment in time.

Becoming more isn't felt with constant applause. Not when you average out the results.

None of us want to be average, right? Most of us want to be *more* than average. Most of want to *experience* more than average. I don't know anyone who would tell their boss they're aiming for an average performance this year. I've not met the person who would go into a restaurant and expect just average service and food quality.

Our personal aspirations also tend to be more than average, In fact, they're often closer to exceptional. There are countless role models who remind us how much potential we all have to be exceptional:

"Don't say you don't have enough time. You have exactly the same number of hours per day that were given to Helen Keller, Pasteur, Michelangelo, Mother Teresa, Leonardo da Vinci, Thomas Jefferson, and Albert Einstein"

– *H. Jackson Brown Jr*

We all have our personal role models, those individuals that we would aspire to be like, whether it's in business, science, arts or sports. They may be a "superstar" in their field or just someone you know or work with personally. Either way, we all have individuals who we aspire to be like, their achievements inspire us towards greatness.

The problem is when we look up to such role models we tend to only focus on the greatness of their achievements, not the accompanying failures they experienced.

Thomas Edison changed the world with the invention of the lightbulb, but not before he experienced a huge number of failures and aborted attempts. Indeed, before he achieved success with the lightbulb, he had worked on hundreds of other ideas and patents that never amounted to anything. They all failed. Whilst the one thing he achieved was exceptional, if you took an average of Edison's success rate as an inventor, it wouldn't look all that impressive.

For all the brilliant theories Einstein published about physics, there were many others that were discarded. We don't focus on Rembrandt's discarded sketch books; we stand in awe of what hangs on the gallery wall.

More often than not, greatness is a moment in time preceded by many other moments of failure, or average performance at best. And yet we (and the history books) tend only to remember and revere the successes, the hits, the moments of greatness.

The problem is, when we only acknowledge the moments of greatness achieved by our role models it can lead us to experience a sense of inadequacy: perhaps we are not good enough to achieve greatness. That's because we're judging our own average against the role model's greatest achievements – perhaps even a single great achievement. When we seek to draw such a comparison we are not doing a "like for like" comparison.

If you compare yourself to some of the great achievers out there, remember that you weren't with them every step of the way. You didn't see the moments they failed, the moments they feared it was impossible, the moments they regretted, the moments when they felt embarrassed by their own lack of ability. But you are with you every step of the way. So perhaps the most important lesson we can take from the great achievers, and from our role models, is that we wouldn't even know their names right now if they had given up when they were failing or experiencing self-doubt.

Maybe your moment of greatness is going to happen after many moments of "less than" greatness. Maybe your goals will take more time to achieve than you expect, or want. Maybe they'll never happen in the way that you hope.

Just don't worry too much about your average; some of the world's greatest achievers also had quite average results if you look at the whole.

But despite their average, they became more than what they were when they started. It is exactly the same for you, you can become more.

It is also important to recognise that when you do become more, especially if your journey involves working for yourself and quitting the day job, it comes with its own pitfalls.

Because when you truly embrace becoming more, with all the accountability and ownership for your own life, you also have to be the one to keep pushing yourself forward.

Whatever your goals and dreams are, ask yourself this question: who are you doing it for?

Who are you accountable to?
Who is your boss?
Who appraises you?
Who determines your worth?

Maybe your moment of greatness is going to happen after many moments of "less than" greatness. Maybe your goals will take more time to achieve than you expect, or want. Maybe they'll never happen in the way that you hope.

Often, it can be easy to complain about "the boss", but let's face it, work has a massive impact on how you feel. And I've not met anyone who doesn't like to get the occasional thanks from the boss, or feel pride when someone recognises they've done a good job. Even if they're the CEO.

But it can be difficult getting the balance right; between feeling assured you're doing the right thing and being your own judge, whilst also acting as part of a wider organisation.

Several years ago my husband made the brave decision to leave his job after 16 years and become self-employed, to 'live the dream', as it were. At first that sense of relief, of being out of the system, was amazing. No more appraisals, no more performance ratings, no more calibration of 'scores'.

But the realisation soon came that all that stuff didn't matter anyway. What really mattered – *all* that really matters – is the rating we give ourselves, every day when we look in the mirror, when we undertake our tasks, when we do our job. Whatever that job may be.

If you feel that you are doing it for someone else, and not for yourself, then it's time to either change how you feel, or change the job.

Whatever your job is, you will be more successful if you feel you are working for yourself. Either be an entrepreneur and lead and manage your own business, *or* be an intrapreneur, working for someone else but under your own motivation, under your own initiative, adding as much value to that organisation as you possibly can.

Because when you add value to that business, you add value to yourself and your future, even if they lie outside of the business or the role you are currently in. It's about recognising the freedom you have, to lead yourself. It's about accepting that you always have choices and one of those choices is maximising your potential and creating opportunities up ahead for yourself.

Whenever you get up and go to work, you should always be doing it for yourself. It should always be about you. Be the best you that you can possibly be and enjoy it.

And if you're reading this on a Friday and feeling grateful for the weekend, remember that you get to live throughout the whole week, not just Saturday and Sunday. If you feel that you only get a life at the weekend, then something needs to change.

It's your life, your happiness, your choice.

When you truly become more you realise that how you feel about your success is up to you, how you feel about your job is up to you. How you feel about your dreams and what you want to do about them, is up to you.

That is when you have become more, when you embrace that exciting, but often scary, notion that you can, will and do live the life you want.

Chapter Ten – the three Rs...

Reflect:

How excited are you about your life? How many times do you find yourself getting energised by the amazing potential your life has? How open are you to the possibilities that lie ahead of you? How much do you feel you are working for yourself, or a slave to a job you don't enjoy?

Respond:

Make a commitment to yourself now to be more mindful of your responses to the circumstances you find yourself in, your job, the reaction to your boss, the tasks you do, the failures you experience. To become more is to realise that your response and subsequent action is a choice.

Result:

You'll know it when you feel it! The feeling of freedom that comes with becoming more, the feeling that you are accountable only to yourself, that you are not trapped in or stuck in a rut. You may still be in the job you don't enjoy, but you will feel less impacted by it. You will be emotionally charged at the end of the day to continue in your pursuit of the life you want to live.

chapter ELEVEN

Now what?

"The time is now..."

"No time like the present..."

"Just do it..."

Familiar phrases all, often used with the intention to inspire, with a hope that they will promote and propel people to act. Such phrases impress on us that the only time to act is now, that the present moment is where you live your life and that is where you can impact it most.

But exactly when is "now"?

The German psychologist and neuroscientist Ernst Poppël suggests that our perception of the present moment, of "now", is a period of time three seconds long. That's a small packet of time. By four seconds we are starting to experience the past, and a mere one or two seconds is perceived to be our future.

Of course, as soon as we've opened our packet of time and gobbled down the three seconds of "now" we're onto the next, and the next, and the next... The three seconds constantly refreshes so we have no perception that "now" is only three seconds long.

Sometimes it is easy to over-analyse and over-plan our lives. We plan in great detail the huge decisions, the grand actions and the big activities associated with our goals and dreams. But in reality it's just about the next three seconds. On repeat. That's your life. And the choices we make in the "now" have the power to significantly impact our entire lives. That's because your entire life is only ever experienced in the three seconds of now!

When you sit and recall happier times your mind is actually recreating those memories, during the three seconds of now, it isn't that you are remembering something that has occurred in the past, but is being recreated in your mind in the present.

When you dream of a better future, that dream is being experienced now.

There is no escaping that the time is always now, and your ability to impact your life, achieve your dreams, work towards a goal or target is, and will always be, now.

Now is when you make choices, now is when you act, now is when you live.

Now is you, and now is everyone else.

The present moment – the *right now* – connects you with every other human being on the planet. It doesn't matter if they are on the other side of the world or sitting right beside you; billions of human beings are existing, living, hoping and dreaming, just like you. Right now. Geography divides, making us feel distant and disconnected, but time brings us all together. Consider how everyone can remember where they were when...

There are so many 'whens'. Celebratory and happy 'whens', such as the turning of the millennium or seeing a particular nation triumph in the World Cup, as well as sad and sobering 'whens', such as acts of terror or natural disasters. Whatever the 'when', such moments in time have the power to unite us. We experience life together, not separated by geography and immediate concerns. Those moments stay with us throughout our lives; they shape who we are and who we become.

We often think of time as flowing like a river, on which we travel from the past through the present and into our future. But perhaps it's more that our boat is anchored to the present, and the water passes beneath us. We don't move, we always remain in the moment.

The past and the future, even when they seem as close as yesterday and tomorrow, are distant and unreachable places. And yet they're important places: the past benefits from reflection and provides learning whilst the future is enriched by our dreams and goals. It is in the present that we shape both the past and the future. But we can also lose the present by being too occupied with what has gone before or what lies ahead.

The present moment not only has the ability to bring you together with all of humanity, it has the ability to bring you together with your whole self.

Being grateful for who you are right now, for where you are right now. Being happy with yourself right now is not only the best gift you can give yourself, but it is the best way to impact your past and future self.

Time is out of your control. It will keep moving and you will keep noticing its incessant impact. It is impossible to escape and, no matter how hard you try, you will never have more time. So maybe it's time to drop the concept of 'having time', or 'making time' or 'no time'; the only part of time you are close to, that you occupy and that you can control is *right now*. Grounded in the present moment, it is only the right now that really matters. Because it is only in the right now that you exist.

Of course many of our goals and dreams have definite beginnings and endings, but both the start and the finish only occur in the present moment. Right now you will be experiencing some beginnings, and possibly some endings, and everyone wants a fairy tale-style happy ending, right, just like in the movies.

Everything turns out as planned, for the best, everyone's happy, dreams are achieved. Movies are great at creating the perfect happy ending, against all odds, where it all just "comes together" in the closing scene.

In real life we too want happy endings, our dreams achieved, challenges overcome, happiness secured. However, real life is not the same as a movie; we have two big stumbling blocks:

How do you define happy?

When exactly is the ending?

Happiness tends to be far more complicated and elusive in real life than in a movie. Nothing is ever really perfect; there will always be some lingering issue or concern. The stuff the characters presumably have to deal after the credits roll and the movie theatre gets cleaned up ready for the next showing.

And what is an ending in our lives? The end of the week, the month, the holiday, the wedding, the big event…?

Maybe we need to let go of the concept of a happy ending, especially when it comes to our goals and dreams. Maybe the burden of a happy ending is weighing heavily on our minds and, as it can never really be achieved in life (as the only *real* ending is death), it can make us feel that we haven't achieved our dreams.

Or worse, we do achieve them, but have some expectation that they are going to deliver some change that never materialises.

An ending suggests something is finished – done, complete. But in life, we are never finished, done and complete – we go on, we wake up the day after our "happy ending" and have to get on with the day to day details of our lives, some of which hardly seem appropriate to the happy ending we've just achieved.

Perhaps the biggest problem with the concept of happy endings is that we believe the external achievement will drive an internal change. That the happy ending will make a big difference to how we feel about ourselves and the world around us.

Aiming for a goal is great, having dreams are brilliant, I'm a huge advocate of this. I've achieved so many of my own personal goals and dreams, but I've also learned that some of the expectations I placed on the achievement of such goals didn't deliver the internal change that I was hoping for.

We hope that when we hit a target weight we will feel better, when we get the job we really want everything will fall into place, when we have the bank balance we've always dreamed of, or the car or the house...

These are all external changes, life achievements. Important of course, but external.

Happiness is not external, it is a state of mind, which requires an internal change, a shift in mind-set. When you can appreciate yourself and find internal happiness with who you are and what you want, you realise that it's *not* about happy endings.

Perhaps the biggest problem with the concept of happy endings is that we believe the external achievement will drive an internal change.

That the happy ending will make a big difference to how we feel about ourselves and the world around us.

It's accepting your happiness as part of a continuation of exploring your potential and living the life you want to live. Accepting that things don't always turn out as we want, that there is still hard work to do, and that we will always have the bad days and weeks ahead of us.

Endings are continuous, you've just ended another minute, day, month and year of your life, depending on where you mark your calendar. When you realise that life is full of endings, full of beginnings, full of potential, full of happiness and sadness, you realise you can create your happy continuations every single day.

Keep being you, keep being fabulous. Live the life you want, just don't expect the external to drive your internal happiness.

And please, I beg you, don't waste a minute of your life. Don't waste it on being apathetic towards yourself, others and the world around you. Don't be numb, drifting through your life as though you are a passenger waiting for someone to else to tell you "this is your stop".

Don't waste a minute with negative self-destroying thoughts, with fear of failure and hatred towards who or what you feel you are.

Don't use aspirational goals to beat yourself up about how unhappy you are with your life, if you want to change it then change it. If you find you can't change it then change how you respond to it.

It isn't about being a constant state of elation, we are only human, of course we will have bad days, bad weeks, maybe even a bad month or two. And everyone is entitled to waste a bit of time now and again, in the same way you're entitled to waste a bit of money on a purchase you don't really need.

But the reason I stress so much about not wasting time, of embracing the possibility and living the life you want, is because when you think about it, we don't even exist.

The universe has been around for a long, *long* time. Our most up to date estimates place the age of the universe at 13.8 billion years old.

The vast space of the universe is also really, *really* big. Perhaps Douglas Adams summed it up best:

Space is big. Really big. You just won't believe how vastly, hugely, mindbogglingly big it is. I mean, you may think it's a long way down the road to the chemist, but that's just peanuts to space...

– Douglas Adams – "The Hitchhikers Guide to The Galaxy"

By comparison, we humans are all rather tiny…

Our size and significance, when compared to the unimaginable scale of the universe, couldn't even be compared to a grain of sand sitting next to an object the size of the earth. In fact, we would be even smaller than the electrons within the atoms that make up a grain of sand sitting next to an object the size of the earth.

Compared to the size of the universe, we're so small that you would struggle to notice or observe our existence at all.

The same applies for the amount of time we each occupy. If the universe is 13,800,000,000 years old and we are lucky enough to live to 80, then by comparison we've occupied 0.00000058% of the universe's history. Statistically, something that is six zeros below zero (such as 0.00000058), is considered to be zero. It is statistically nothing.

So when you consider the enormous space and time of the universe and compare that to the space and time we occupy, our lives are inexpressibly brief.

I'm not wanting to depress you with this information – in fact I'd like it to uplift and liberate you.

Consider how precious, unique and fleeting your life is; we have such a tiny window of opportunity to live our lives, to identify and fulfil our dreams and purpose, that we should seize every opportunity.

If we embrace the notion that we exist for only the merest fraction of a blink in time and space, then delaying the pursuit of anything we want begins to make no sense at all.

Don't wait.

Don't doubt yourself. Don't let fear and self-criticism get in the way. Don't let others tell you that you can't or that you shouldn't. Don't settle for less. Don't let others tell you that you shouldn't be wanting more. Don't allow yourself to have a bored weekend where you feel you have nothing to do.

If our lives are so small and so brief that we barely exist, then I dare you to be noticed. I dare you to live out your purpose so boldly and radiantly and exuberantly that the universe *will* notice and resonate from the glorious contribution you've made.

Dream more, do more and become more.

CONSIDER HOW PRECIOUS, UNIQUE AND FLEETING YOUR LIFE IS; WE HAVE SUCH A TINY WINDOW OF OPPORTUNITY TO LIVE OUR LIVES, TO IDENTIFY AND FULFIL OUR DREAMS AND PURPOSE, THAT WE SHOULD SEIZE EVERY OPPORTUNITY.

Chapter Eleven – the three Rs...

Reflect:

Considering how brief life is (not in a negative way), how much time have you wasted with negativity? Time wasted fearing failure or embarrassment? Have you become too attached to a vision of a happy ending? Is it in danger of becoming an unbreakable dream?

Respond:

Be active in choosing happiness, commit to look for the positives. Being thankful and grateful on a daily basis has a massive impact to how you feel, and how you feel has in turn a huge impact on continuing to pursue your goals.

Result:

To be continued...

Afterword

I hope that you have enjoyed reading this book and that it has provided you with some inspiration and practical advice on how to live the life you want and achieve your dreams.

As I mentioned throughout the book, some dreams will be harder to achieve than others.

Some dreams will be realised in different shapes and sizes than you had originally imagined.

And there are dreams, goals and amazing achievements ahead of you that you don't even know about yet.

There's no turning back the clock to un-do past choices. You are where you are and who you are. You know what you want and for most part you probably know what you need to do to get it.

You're still going to have bad days, and no inspirational / motivational phrase can change the circumstances you may find yourself in from time to time.

But believe me when I say that you can do what you want to do, you can live the life you want.

Keep being you, keep being fabulous and always want more.

Have fun – Johnathan

THIS PAGE HAS BEEN LEFT
INTENTIONALLY BLANK

22334218R00135

Printed in Great Britain
by Amazon